THE MISHAP LINEAGE

The Mishap Lineage

TRANSFORMING CONFUSION INTO WISDOM

Chögyam Trungpa

Edited by Carolyn Rose Gimian

SHAMBHALA
BOSTON & LONDON
2009

Dedicated to the people of Surmang

Shambhala Publications, Inc.
Horticultural Hall
300 Massachusetts Avenue
Boston, Massachusetts 02115
www.shambhala.com

A portion of the author's proceeds from this book are being donated to the
Konchok Foundation, which supports the rebuilding of the Surmang monasteries,
the education of the Twelfth Trungpa, and other projects in East Tibet.

Frontispiece: Chögyam Trungpa in the robes of the
Tenth Trungpa. Photo by Martin Janowitz.
The Tibetan symbol that appears on the cover and chapter openers of this book
is called an *Evam. Evam* is the personal seal of the Trungpa tulkus. It is
a symbol of the unity of the feminine principle of space and wisdom, *E*,
with the masculine principle of compassion and skillful means, *Vam.*

Printed in the United States of America

♾ This edition is printed on acid-free paper that meets the
American National Standards Institute z39.48 Standard.
♻ Shambhala Publications makes every effort to print on recycled paper.
For more information please visit www.shambhala.com.
Distributed in the United States by Random House, Inc.,
and in Canada by Random House of Canada Ltd

Designed by Gopa & Ted2, Inc.

Library of Congress Cataloging-in-Publication Data
Trungpa, Chögyam, 1939–1987.
The mishap lineage: transforming confusion into wisdom / Chögyam
Trungpa; edited by Carolyn Rose Gimian.—1st ed.
p. cm.
Includes bibliographical references and index.
ISBN 978-1-59030-713-7 (pbk.: alk. paper)
1. Drun-pa lamas—Biography. 2. Religious life—Kar-ma-pa (Sect) I.
Gimian, Carolyn Rose. II. Title.
BQ7682.9.A2T78 2009
294.3'9230922—dc22
[B]
2009008425

Contents

Editor's Preface

THE MISHAP LINEAGE: Transforming Confusion into Wisdom is Chögyam Trungpa's personal reflection on his lineage, the lineage of Trungpa *tulkus*, or incarnate teachers, which began in Tibet in the fifteenth century. Chögyam Trungpa himself, who was born in Tibet in 1940, was the Eleventh Trungpa.[1] In this book, Trungpa Rinpoche—*rinpoche* is a title for reincarnate teachers that means "precious one"—is not so much documenting the history of the teachers in the lineage as he is informing our own contemporary experience with the myths or stories of his predecessors. Here, stories from the lives of the Trungpas are a point of departure for the discussion of the principles and the experiences that guide a practitioner's journey on the path. These discussions are also related to how he viewed the introduction of the Buddhist teachings in North America and his hopes for their future.

He uses the historical framework to help us understand how we can relate to the idea of lineage and community in the modern context of a spiritual journey. What is the nature of lineage? How can we, as twenty-first-century practitioners, connect with the stories of practitioners' experiences hundreds of years ago? Does their experience apply to us? Is it true, is it relevant, is it real? These are questions the reader can explore in this volume. Perhaps some of the questions will be answered. Perhaps some will remain as fuel for the journey. That would certainly be in keeping with how the author taught. He was much more interested in awakening curiosity than in providing certainty, and the style of the presentation here is in keeping with that.

The idea of the Mishap Lineage, encountering and sometimes even inviting constant mishaps and then using them as the ground for the next stage of development on the path, is introduced here as a defining characteristic of the Kagyü lineage, and particularly of the line of the Trungpas. The theme of mishaps and the lineage of mishaps comes up over and over. So far as I was able to uncover, there is no term for "Mishap Lineage" in Tibetan. Chögyam Trungpa gave us dynamic translations for key Buddhist terms in the English language, many of which have shaped the view of practice and the Buddhist path in America. Beyond that, he coined new phrases that have no equivalent in Tibetan or Sanskrit, such as *spiritual materialism, meditation in action,* and—now we learn—*Mishap Lineage.* These terms may be among the most important concepts he presented; clearly, they are particularly applicable to Buddhism in America. The concept of the Mishap Lineage also reflects the personal quality of his own journey. His coming to the West only occurred because of the "mishap" of the Chinese invasion of Tibet. His coming from England to America only took place because of many mishaps that occurred in England. He himself feasted on mishaps, using them as fuel and food for the continuing journey rather than shying away. *The Mishap Lineage* was chosen as the title for this book because this principle seems to resonate so strongly with our experience of Buddhist practice in the West. The seminar that was the basis for much of the material in this book, as far as this editor knows, is the first place where this concept was introduced.

Chögyam Trungpa died more than twenty years ago, on April 4, 1987, yet his teachings are still practiced today by thousands, many of whom never met him, and read each year by tens of thousands more. There is a growing appreciation for the central role that he played in bringing the Buddhist teachings to the West, in particular his pivotal role in establishing the tradition of the Practicing Lineage in America. This book is an offering to him, the teachers of his lineage, and to his students, both those who knew him and studied with him personally, as well as those who encounter him in his written work or are practicing now in his tradition, applying his teachings in their practice of meditation, following the path he laid out.

This volume is also an offering to the current teachers and practitioners at the Surmang monasteries in East Tibet, especially those at Surmang Dütsi Tel, Trungpa Rinpoche's main monastery in Tibet, which his Western students are now helping to rebuild; Kyere Gön, a small monastery not far from Surmang Dütsi Tel, where Rinpoche discovered many important *terma* teachings;[2] and Wenchen Nunnery, near Kyere, where the nuns practice many of Rinpoche's teachings in their retreats. After all, as Rinpoche says in the last talk: "Surmang is Trungpa. Trungpa is Surmang." It is where most of the events described in this volume took place. And we should not forget that without Surmang and the mishaps that affected Tibet, there would never have been a Chögyam Trungpa in America. We owe these people and this place an enormous debt.

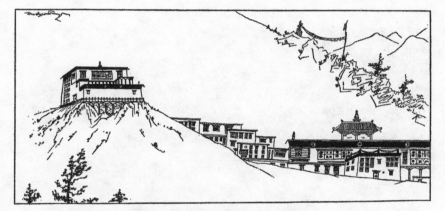

Surmang Dütsi Tel. Drawing by Chögyam Trungpa.

In December 1975, when Rinpoche presented the Mishap Lineage seminar (originally titled "The Line of the Trungpas" seminar) that is the basis for this book, he had little reason to believe that his dharma lineage had survived at Surmang. Rinpoche began his journey out of Tibet in 1959, after receiving a report of the sacking of the monastery. His bursar described to him how the sacred remains of the Tenth Trungpa were desecrated by the Chinese. The bursar, having cremated the remains, brought them to Rinpoche. Understandably, Trungpa Rinpoche saw little future for the dharma in Tibet. Many terma teachings that he had discovered at Surmang were destroyed, as far as he knew, as well as other practice texts and writings. He rarely spoke about these teachings, perhaps in part because he saw no chance that they would be recovered.

Toward the end of his life, Trungpa Rinpoche received letters and other communications from Tibet, including a letter from his mother, and he expressed a desire to visit Surmang by helicopter (since he was not well enough to get there by other means), but this was not to be. Following his death, a number of his students traveled to Surmang and began to reestablish relationships there.[3] In the late 1990s, the first teacher from Surmang Dütsi Tel came to America. Khenpo Tsering Gyurme traveled to Colorado to meet his Western dharma family, to bring us news of our Tibetan dharma brothers and sisters, and to ask for assistance in rebuilding and reenergizing the situation there. In 2003, he worked with the Nalanda

Sakyong Mipham Rinpoche, Chögyam Trungpa's eldest son and lineage holder, conducting a long life empowerment at Surmang, 2004. Photo by Peter G. Seidler.

Translation Committee to bring two other teachers from Surmang to America: Karma Senge Rinpoche (aka Karseng Rinpoche), Trungpa Rinpoche's nephew; and Damchö Tenphel Rinpoche, Trungpa Rinpoche's younger brother. Karseng Rinpoche, who never met Chögyam Trungpa, spent years traveling throughout East Tibet gathering copies of all of the texts that Chögyam Trungpa had written or received as terma during his

*Family portrait from the visit of Diana Mukpo (Chögyam Trungpa's widow)
to Tibet, summer 2002.*

twenty years in Tibet. Karseng Rinpoche received the transmissions for
these texts from practitioners there, who kept their copies of these texts as
their preciously guarded treasures. Now the Nalanda Translation Committee is translating this material, and Rinpoche's students in North America
are beginning to receive these transmissions.[4]

If we could ask him, Trungpa Rinpoche—even knowing that the dharma
tradition in Surmang had survived—would surely still emphasize that a key
component of the future of Buddhism lies in the West. He was a remark-
ably prescient person. His emphasis on the teachings going forward in the
West was not just a response to what had happened in his homeland. While
paying homage to the history of the lineage and with respect and love for
our Asian origins, we must look to ourselves, Western practitioners of the
dharma, to stabilize and carry forward the future of Chögyam Trungpa's
dharma legacy. We must make the teachings our own. Choicelessly, we
carry a responsibility for the propagation of his teachings. What he did in
America was unique, and the burden to preserve that is ours. He trusted
his Western students in a way that is almost beyond comprehension. How
can we not repay that trust?

Nevertheless, we feel humbled by the exertion, devotion, and realization of those teachers we've met from Surmang.[5] More than that, meeting them feels like meeting family. How extraordinary to feel so at home with people from this far, far away place, so different from our own and yet so similar. It is also that sense of meeting family that recurs throughout reading the stories in *The Mishap Lineage*.

During a break while working on this volume in the country outside of Halifax, Nova Scotia, I went for a walk through fields behind the retreat house. It had been a winter with little snow, so although it was only mid-March, most of the snow had melted, and I was able to trudge through the fields of long, unmown hay. In many places, the undergrowth was pushed up in peaks and hillocks by a combination of wind, snow, and animals bedding down in the grass. I was reminded of Trungpa Rinpoche's story about the origin of the name *Surmang*, which means simply "many cornered." The teacher Trung Ma-se took the name *Surmang* from the reed hut in which he lived for many years. The hut had a lot of corners, because you need those if you build a house out of just reeds. Here, centuries later and thousands of miles away, in the fields behind a little house in eastern Canada, I saw hundreds of corners made out of long grass, and it felt as though I were seeing the footprints of the teacher, pushing up the grasses wherever he walked.

In this small volume, may you encounter some of these footprints making a path through your mind and into your heart. May we all benefit from the teachings of the Mishap Lineage.

Carolyn Rose Gimian
Trident Mountain House
Nova Scotia

Ocean Waves of Devotion

A Supplication to the Garland of Births of the
Surmang Trungpa Rinpoches

Supreme lord of the hundred devas of Tushita,
Great Maitreya of great maitri, protector of beings,
Dharma regent, the great prince himself,
We supplicate you, the future buddha.

Born of a royal family, you attained the siddhi of Hevajra;
By the action of a great lord of yogins,
Riding a miraculous tiger, you are victorious in all directions.
We supplicate you, Dombi Heruka.

In the mansion of the luminous vajra pinnacle
Vidyadhara arises in the form of a mahasiddha.
The protector who makes the doctrine of the supreme yana shine like
   the sun,
We supplicate at your feet, Shri Simha.

Heart son, blessed by the great Ugyen,
Who pierced the evil king with a vajra arrow,
Vajrapani disguised as a man,
We supplicate at your feet, Palkyi Dorje.

You accomplished the realization of the nonduality of prana and mind,
Self-liberating all dharmas of samsara and nirvana in mahamudra;
Never passing from there, Truku Repa,
We supplicate you, great lord of siddhas.

You pleased the supreme guru and obtained the profound instructions;
Practicing them correctly, appearance dawned as dharmakaya;
You realized mind as unborn dharmakaya.
We supplicate at your feet, Lhopa Gomchung.

The prince, born from the family of Nyö,
Perfected the great mind-power of completely knowing the sutras
    and tantras,
Exalted on the crest of the ocean of siddhas and pandits.
We supplicate you, Thingma Sanggye Trak.

Heart son of Lodrö Rinchen, mahasiddha of the Practice Lineage,
Greatly empowered with the realization of true meaning,
Completely attaining the dharmakaya kingdom of nonmeditation,
We supplicate at your feet, Kunga Gyaltsen.

You planted the victory banner of practice in the place of Tserlung.
Mahakala has shown you his pleasing face again and again.
Supreme commander of the ocean of ability and power,
We supplicate at your feet, Kunga Sangpo.

Outwardly, completely caring for the practice of a shravaka,
Inwardly, mind steeped with the two bodhichittas,
Secretly, binding all dharmas of samsara and nirvana in the avadhuti,
We supplicate at your feet, Kunga Öser.

Seeing clearly all the vast knowable dharmas of the universe,
Holding still the essence of prana, nadi, and bindu,
Great chief of the siddhas of Chakrasamvara and others,
We supplicate at your feet, Kunga Namgyal.

Exalted amidst the ocean of the Practice Lineage,
Perfect in learning, contemplation, and meditation, you attained
    their essence
And accomplished the siddhi of samyag-jnana.
We supplicate at your feet, Tenpa Namgyal.

All the rivers of the four oral lineages
Are gathered in your mind's ocean—you ripen disciples
And have reached the highest mark of the paths and stages.
We supplicate you, Tendzin Chökyi Gyatso.

Wealthy in the treasure of the ocean of the hearing lineage,
Raising the jewel victory banner of the two siddhis,
The friend who leads worthy ones on the good path of the four kayas,
We supplicate you, Jampal Chökyi Gyatso.

Supreme among the million holders of the Karma Kagyü doctrine,
Fully manifesting the mark of the path that achieves the profound
    secret,
Completely holding the powerful force of buddha activity, which
    benefits others,
We supplicate at your feet, Gyurme Tenphel.

You who became the heart son of Karmapa,
With the eye that sees the ultimate teaching just as it is,
Lord of dharma, you spread the hearing lineage, which ripens and frees.
We supplicate at your feet, Tenpa Rabgye.

Only heart son of the Jamyang guru,
Resplendent leader of siddhas and pandits,
Holding the life-force of the Karma Kagyü doctrine,
We supplicate at your feet, Chökyi Nyinche.

Lord of yogins—Kunga Lekpa and so on—
In the play of the million siddhas and pandits of the old and new schools,

You possess the mind that recalls previous existences.
We supplicate you, all-pervading lord, the glorious guru.

Prince, great moon of compassion,
You spread the power of the enlightened family,
Showing the great yana, the good path of the Victorious One.
We supplicate you, Karma Thrinle Künkhyap.

Likewise, to the assembly of root and lineage gurus,
We respectfully prostrate, make offerings, confess evil deeds and
    degrading actions;
Rejoicing in virtue, we request you to turn the wheel of dharma;
We request you to remain, not passing into nirvana, and we dedicate
    the accumulation of virtue.

May the multitude of beings stretching to the limits of the sky
Purify obscurations, perfect the accumulations, and attain the state of
    the four kayas.
From today onwards, until I and others attain the essence of
    enlightenment,
May the glorious guru accept us and never be separated from us.

*At the request of Karma Ösal Lhüntrup, who holds the treasure of the three
disciplines, I, Jamyang Chökyi Lodrö, wrote this so that the blessings of the
guru may seep into your heart.* SARVADA MANGALAM[1]

CHAPTER ONE

The Practicing Lineage

T HE SUBJECT of this book is the Trungpa lineage, or the line of
the Trungpas. The author of this book belongs to this lineage. He
is one of the Trungpas. In fact, I am the eleventh one of them.
We are not talking about the dynasty of a kingdom, and we are not talking about a family history. But we are talking about *how* the lineage situation evolved through the various Trungpas over the ages, up to the present
situation.

The first question is, what particular tradition is the line of the Trungpas
associated with? To begin with, Buddhism, of course, and then the Buddhist tradition in Tibet. What kind of Buddhist discipline is associated
with the Trungpa lineage? And what particular locality of Tibet is the lineage connected to? We are forced to consider the background story, which
is connected with what is known as the "teachings of the Practicing Lineage." All of you who are reading this book and studying these teachings
are also part of that lineage. At this point, a lot of you have inherited it, a
lot of you are just about to inherit it, and a lot of you are just beginning to
dip into this particular tradition. That tradition, again, is called the "Practicing Lineage."

There are four major schools of Tibetan Buddhism. These are the old,
or older, school; the medium, or middle, schools; and the newest one. The
old school is known as the Nyingma tradition. It is continuing the tradition of Padmasambhava, the great Buddhist adept, saint, and yogi who

formally, officially introduced, or instigated, the teachings of Buddha into Tibet from India. Then there are the medium, or middle, schools, which are two: the Kagyü and the Sakya. They came into the picture much later, presenting further Buddhist teachings from India. Then, the latest one, the newest one, the youngest one of all, is the Geluk tradition.

The Geluk tradition is, we could say, completely and fully a Tibetan product of Buddhism, because it did not have any direct historical relationship to Indian Buddhism. At the time that the Geluk tradition arose, Indian Buddhism was already far gone and slowly dying out, due to the Moslem invasions of India. Most of the remaining Buddhists in India were persecuted or had gone underground. A lot of the Buddhist monasteries were attacked by the Moslems, because the Moslem troops thought that people wearing uniforms must be soldiers. So monks were killed and monasteries were completely destroyed.

The Islamic tradition, particularly, doesn't believe in making idols out of any deities. They believe that any images representing the truth shouldn't be anthropomorphic. Consequently, the Moslems destroyed many Buddhist statues, wiping out evidence of Buddhist culture as much as they could. Still to this day, from excavations taking place in India, we are finding Buddhist temples, *stupas*, and images that have received a token Moslem seal on them: either the statue is without a nose, or without ears or fingers, as a mark of disapproval of the deification of anthropomorphic images.[1]

To get back to the main subject, the Practicing Lineage is one of the middle schools, the Kagyü, which came after the old, or ancient, schools. The Kagyü lineage developed through various Tibetan masters—scholars who visited India and received teachings there and then returned to establish their particular situation in Tibet. Namely, there was the famous translator-saint Marpa, who visited India three times and brought the teachings he received there to Tibet. His disciple Milarepa was the greatest yogic poet of Tibet, or shall we say, singer-poet. We could call him the first Tibetan blues singer. And then there was his disciple Gampopa, and then Gampopa's descendants established the lineage of the Karmapas. At this point, the lineage of the Kagyü, the Practicing Lineage, consists of something like forty-five generations—up to the time of the Eleventh Trungpa, whoever he might be!

The meaning and significance of the Practicing Lineage is important for you to understand before we can consider the rest of the story, so to speak. *Practicing Lineage* is a term that was developed by Milarepa. Previously, the tradition was known as the "Lineage of the Sacred Word," which is actually a phrase that we are using again these days. In the Kagyü tradition, *ka* means "Logos," "sacred word," "command," "truth," and *gyü* means "thread" or "continuity"—which is close to the idea of lineage. In Milarepa's time, the Kagyü tradition became known as "Drubgyü": *drub* means "practice," and *gyü* means "lineage" or "line." The Practicing Lineage places a lot of importance on the necessity to practice, to sit or meditate. Without practicing, without understanding the meaning of practice, no *real* communication or development takes place in your understanding of Buddhism, or the buddhadharma.

In the Practicing Lineage, it is equally important to have a great deal of devotion to your teacher, who actually embodies the symbolism or the concept of practice. The guru himself or herself has already achieved a high degree of enlightenment through practice. Moreover, the guru is the only person who can actually push you and who can be a heavy-handed friend, who can actually make you sit a lot and go beyond your slothfulness and laziness. If you want to boycott anything, only the guru can push you and make you sit a lot, practice a lot.

Theoretically, a cosmic guru could send you blessings and encouragements through your psychic antenna, and he might tell you all kinds of stories and send you all kinds of messages. Such things are regarded as very fishy according to the Practicing Lineage. We can always reinterpret such messages according to our own desires. To begin with, our own interpretations, received through our antennae, are not so substantial. But on top of that, we can actually reinterpret things according to our liking.

So it is necessary that the guru be an earthly person, born and raised on this planet earth, to begin with. You need someone who regards himself or herself as a human being, who would like to share the love and hate, sweet and sour, and hot and cold of this particular world. It must be someone who can speak to you on a person-to-person basis, who acts as a mirror reflection, in some sense, and also provides real, genuine communication, independent of politicking or over-indulgence in either charitable kindness or obsession with masochistic trips. The guru-student relationship must be free from all those things. It requires someone who is somewhat sensible, reasonable, but at the same time unyielding. Traditionally, this is a wise person, somebody who can't be persuaded to buy your side, or your trip. It must be somebody who can actually be clear about the whole thing, somebody who buys your story with a pinch of salt, but at the same time is kind and friendly—to a certain extent. Such a person is the teacher, who then teaches you to practice a lot, to sit and meditate a lot.

The basic teachings of Buddha are about understanding what we are, who we are, why we are. When we begin to realize what we are, who we are, why we are, then we begin to realize what we are *not*, who we are *not*, why we are *not*. We begin to realize that we don't have basic, substantial, solid, fundamental ground that we can exert anymore. We begin to realize that our ideas of security and our concept of freedom have been purely phantom experiences.

We would like to use spiritual discipline and traditional wisdom to fit into our own particular pigeonholes, our own desires. We usually want to glorify ourselves by collecting stories and wisdom from every worthy person. We would like to meet lots of people who are seemingly worthy people according to our own judgment, and we constantly collect all of those stories and re-edit them according to what we want. When we begin to do that, we develop our own version of freedom, which is, "I would like to become a greater version of myself, spiritually uplifted, and so forth. I might even have a special place in social situations, be known as an important wise person, so that people will come to me and consult me." We have those kinds of desires. We are not really interested in developing spiritually; we are more interested in evolving politically in the name of spirituality. Such a situation is known as "spiritual materialism." I actually wrote a book about it, called *Cutting Through Spiritual Materialism*. The Practicing Lineage teaches us that we have to get rid of those ego-centered conceptualized notions of the grandiosity of our own development. If we are truly involved with spirituality, we are willing to let go of trying to witness our own enlightenment, the celebration of our enlightenment. One can't watch one's own burial, in other words. We have to learn to be willing to die, to subside. This particular "me" that wanted to attain enlightenment has to go away. When that happens, then you actually attain enlightenment.

In order to shed the ego, in order to understand the principle of egolessness, we have to practice a lot, sit a lot. We have to *experience* a lot. We might have some intellectual, analytical understanding, but even that understanding has to be based on an intuitive experience of the practice situation. Without that, we can't develop at all. We are simply creating and expanding further schemes related to our own grand plans for a spiritual ego trip, spiritual materialism, and so forth.

Everyone in the lineage of the practicing tradition has been extremely sarcastic and critical of the current scenes taking place around them. They were extremely critical of the subtle corruption taking place in the name of the dharma. We could say that the Practicing Lineage is the guardian of the buddhadharma, not only in Tibet alone but in the rest of the world. Someone should at least have a critical view of how things should happen, how things shouldn't happen. That particular sharp vision, traditionally known as "*prajna* vision," is very important. And that is a very lively situation, a living situation, which still is up-to-date. In fact, that is why we are here.

The Practicing Lineage is the most pure, and is unhampered by any kind of spiritual materialism. Instead of just viewing this lineage from a purely historical point of view, we should realize that this experience of lineage can take place in ourselves.

How we have come to be, how we have come to practice—our particular basic, general background—is that we would like to become richer and more conscious people, highly evolved people. That is why we are interested in spiritual practice. That is our "trip," and those trips are known as real *trips*.[2] Those trips are questionable, and such trips require a very heavy critical dosage of the Practicing Lineage message, so that we can be woken up from our naïveté, our confused attitude about spirituality, and our attempts to pollute the spiritual world of the current century.[3]

Student: Is the desire to be more aware always problematic?

Chögyam Trungpa Rinpoche: It seems that way. That very word *desire* makes the whole thing questionable. However, there is a difference between desiring to be more aware and being willing to be more aware. If you're just willing, it's very straightforward. But if you *desire* to be, and you are *trying* to be, and you're trying to reach some degree of reference point, that seems to be problematic.

S: Have you ever experienced a desire to spread Buddhism in the West, or is it just a willingness?

CTR: Both.

S: I'm curious to know what happens next when you experience the desire?

CTR: Well, if you are at the point of being willing to spread Buddhism and having your desire be for Buddhism, I don't see any particular problems. When you get into Buddhism completely, you have the capability of spreading the teachings. I wouldn't exactly equate that with the desire such as Hitler or Mussolini had. It seems to be a slightly different kettle of fish. Spreading the dharma is such a big undertaking that you can't make it your show, your private project. You can't have a large-scale personal desire anymore. You are basically intimidated [by how huge the project is]. You could try to use guns and bullets, as a Hitler or a Mussolini might do, but that is quite contradictory in spreading Buddhism. You also can't use too many pamphlets, and you can't spread the dharma in the style of Billy Graham, either. Spreading the dharma is not a situation of emotionally invoking the teachings. Buddhism is very dull. You have to be willing to come across all kinds of obstacles. If you are willing to take such chances, quite possibly you're willing to be fearless at the same time. At the point where you've reached the level of fearlessness, your desire has somewhat subsided.

CTR: Somebody else? Resident poet? [*Laughter*]

Allen Ginsberg: Does meditation tend naturally to cut through ambition?

CTR: I think so, unless you are in some kind of an endurance contest. That happens in some American Zen traditions. But I think fundamentally it should and could and would.

S: Is there any way that a person can hope to share something he's found that he thinks is of value, with his friends or his family, without getting manipulative and into a power thing?

CTR: Absolutely. This is what the essence of compassion is, you know: to copy how you relate with your child. I think the question is how much you want to be the head of the family or the ringleader of your friends. You know, if that ambition is not there, but you have a genuine willingness to share, that is precisely the concept of *sangha*, in traditional terms. You are willing to be friends with everybody, but at the same time you are not particularly taking credit. You don't make people depend on you. Everybody can stand on his or her own feet. The idea of helping is to make others independent of you. You help them to become more independent rather than making them addicted to you. Those are the two kinds of help. As long as that understanding is clear, there's no problem. The whole thing is delightful.

S: Rinpoche, as one's practice deepens, one becomes more and more aware of spiritual materialism, to the point that one experiences it so much that one reaches a state of complete nausea. How can this be used as an inspiration to go on?
CTR: I think we have to go slightly further and then stop there. You see what I mean?
S: You mean by welcoming the feeling? By acknowledging it?
CTR: Not necessarily. But you're still willing to face further icebergs.
S: Further what?
CTR: Icebergs. Then the whole thing is terrific. [*Laughter*]
S: Is that a promise?
CTR: If you like. Great icebergs. [*Laughter*] It's a very cold promise.

S: I've heard you talk several times about the guru being a mirror to the students. I'd like you to say something more about that.
CTR: Well, I think I've said enough. Maybe if I say too much, the guru ceases to be a mirror. He becomes a tape recorder.
S: Gotcha.

S: One thing I was wondering about was political ambition in the name of spirituality and how that connects with some kind of political scene. This would also dampen one's naive notions about spirituality.

CTR: I think people would like to build themselves up into important people who can manipulate others, starting with their friends, and finally including the rest of the world. Whenever the ego orientation is to make the whole thing grand, that is related with a power trip, shall we say, which becomes political.

S: I see a lot of people personally getting carried away with some small sense of power that they may have in a spiritual community. Sometimes I wonder what the balancing factor is. Who keeps on top of them?

CTR: Well, I don't think the whole thing works that way, particularly. It doesn't have to be that somebody keeps on top of them or that the whole situation is purely a computerized system of levels of bureaucracy. We could say that the whole situation is based on natural evolution, in some sense.

Sometimes a person would like to exert his or her power in practicing spirituality in order to develop further grandiosity, glorifying his or her own existence. That is quite transparent, which is to say that in this situation people are not actually in keeping with the lineage heritage. They would like to step out of it and create their own little satellite, which is known as an unguided missile.

However, we can't lay a trip on a head cook who has to lay a trip on the rest of the cooks in a kitchen. We can't lay a trip on the head garbageman who is laying trips on the rest of the garbage crew, or the head builder who is laying trips on the rest of the builders. Those are not particularly regarded as spiritual trips. They are necessary trips, in order to make things happen. There has to be a central headquarters of information that is redistributed or passed on to others. And since your question was by innuendo, my answer could also be by innuendo. [*Laughter*]

I would like to encourage everyone to sit and practice meditation. If you don't do that, you are creating further pollution and further problems. If you haven't practiced meditation before, you might experience some difficulties, both physical problems and problems with boredom. Such things are purely petty problems. If you are willing to go ahead and practice, you can do it. I would very highly encourage you to take part in the sitting practice of meditation. In that way, you create further purity in your life situation, rather than further pollution.

CHAPTER TWO

Kagyü Lineage / Mishap Lineage

W E COULD GO further in understanding the meaning of the contemplative tradition and why the tradition that I come from, the Practicing Lineage or the Kagyü lineage, exists. It is not just an accident or a matter of chance. Rather, the whole thing is somewhat planned or programmed, to the extent that there is an intelligent awareness or a vision at work as to how a practitioner's lineage can exist and continue.

As far as that vision is concerned, lineage is a prolonged sense of commitment to humanity and to working with the neurosis of humanity. The Practicing Lineage is not based on practitioners locking themselves up in their meditation cells so that they become social nuisances. But practitioners in our lineage work with their commitment to their teacher and with surrendering, openness, and devotion altogether, which is their commitment to the rest of the world: all sentient beings.

Usually, when we practice some kind of discipline and we begin to teach that discipline to others, we tend to present a great number of personal qualifications and credentials, hoping that they will carry us a long way. After that, we just say what we have to say, which is quite short and maybe presented with the pretense of some kind of wit, which is based on not having enough confidence in oneself. So the whole thing short-circuits. That is the usual style of presentation for somebody without any background or lineage. Traditionally that has been a problem. But in this case, borrowing the name of the lineage is not so important in order to reach people. It is not so much proving one's credentials or using them as one's own decorations. Rather, the point is to tell people that their lineage had good forefathers and that there is a good background, a good lineage, *behind* them. So it is a trustworthy situation.

Similarly, the Kagyü tradition has developed more pride in an individual's practice and less quotation from the lineage as a reference point. People relate with practice much more closely, but not in the Ram Dass fashion, which is a mutual confession:[1] "I'm fucked up, you're fucked up, so let's meet together and have a nice time and talk it over." But in this case, let us meet each other in the spirit of the Practitioner's Lineage. Let us encourage each other to sit, let us practice together. Let us encourage each other properly, fully, thoroughly, so that we can inspire ourselves in the spirit of *awake* rather than in the spirit of confusion. When that begins to happen, there is lots of room to expand.

Traditionally, it is said that Kagyüpas and goats like to preside over rocky mountains, and Gelukpas and horses like to roam around in the fields. That is an interesting saying. The reason the Kagyüpas would like to preside over rocky mountains is partially that we are mountain freaks, traditionally and geographically, and partially we would like to approach things from the hard-core practitioner's angle—in a very personal style.

You might ask, "If your particular tradition is so interested in locking yourselves up in caves and practicing by yourselves, how is it possible to expand your administration? How can administration and expansiveness take place all together?" That is a very interesting point, which you should understand. It's a very important point here. Although the Kagyüpas like to live in the rocks in the mountains, they don't particularly make a nest in the mountains, the rocks, and the caves. They conquer the mountains and the rocks. They don't regard their caves as hippie pads or as apartments where they can indulge themselves. You have no idea what goes on in the rest of the apartment building, but you have a nice little cave on the fifth or sixth floor. In this case, it is conquering the whole mountain.

Likewise, the Kagyüpas are known for conquering foreign territory. The rings of Kagyüpa expansion took place not only within the heart of Tibet alone, but the Kagyüpas also liked to live in the territories. The Kagyüpas established rings of expansion into Bhutan, Sikkim—which is on the border of Tibet—and India. They also expanded into the Xinjiang Province of China, into Mongolia, and all the rest of the countries bordering Tibet. The Kagyüpas are not afraid of the cliffs or sheer drops of cultural misunderstanding that exist. If you jump from one culture to another, you may find that the next culture does not have any connections with you. You find that jumping into another country is like jumping off another cliff. But the Kagyüpas never feared that. And likewise we are here now in America. We are not afraid of foreign space. Foreign space is domestic space at the same time.

The expansion of the Practicing Lineage is interesting. It sheds light on Buddhism altogether, in some sense. The southern tradition of Buddhism had reservations about conquering the mountains. So the hinayana tradition went to the south, into Southeast Asia.[2] The *vajrayana* tradition went to northern India, crossing the barbarian lands. The Indians used to call Tibet the "monkey land" or the "vampire land," "the land of red-faced people who eat raw meat and drink raw milk," which was regarded by the Indians as a terrible thing to do. From their point of view, to have never known vegetables is absolutely terrible.

The Kagyü tradition also developed a sense of fearlessness. We often find that relating with our own bodies and minds is a foreign situation as well. We are confronted with foreign territories constantly, again and again, all the time. We are always faced with the unknown. Our death, our birth, our parents, our emotionality: everything is always a foreign country. And *that* mountain, *that* foreign territory is also conquered in the Kagyü tradition, as much as the physical geographical territory beyond Tibet has been conquered.

You might say this is such Kagyü chauvinism. I think that is true. But behind such chauvinism, there is an immense sense of devotion. With that hard-core conquering of the mountains and conquering foreign territory, at the same time there is also an immense sense of softness, surrendering, and sentimentality. The Kagyü tradition is based on sentimentality—of a higher level, of course. [*Laughter*] It is not so much the sentimentality of dreaming about one's mother's chicken soup when you're hungry, or thinking about a well-made kreplach or Christmas pudding, for that matter.

An interesting thing develops by being emotional and hard-core at the same time. We don't usually connect those things together. We don't usually smoke menthol cigarettes and Marlboros at once. [*Laughter*] But they could be blended together. That is what the Kagyü tradition is actually doing. The hard core of relating with the foreignness of foreignness of foreignness exists all the time in our life. You pay your landlord the rent, and you think that at least you can relax for a month. Suddenly, the landlord knocks on your door and says, "I want to kick you out, because you did such and such a thing. Leave. Otherwise, I'm going to call the police." Or you think that your love affair is going well. Suddenly, something comes up. Your lover has apparently not spoken out enough, and suddenly the pimple begins to burst. A big explosion takes place.

All kinds of things like that take place in our life. We think we have settled or solved our most outrageous or outstanding problem. Whew. We try to relax. Then something else comes up and scares us. We might think that we know New York City completely, inside out—which street not to go on, which areas to avoid. But we get mugged on Fifth Avenue or in the United Nations' building. That is always possible. Such things happen to us all the time. So we find that we can't actually relax to the extent we thought, and we can't be caught up in our situation completely or up in arms all the time, either. There's room for romanticism and as well there's room for working with foreign territory all the time.

The Kagyü tradition begins to teach us that. We experience, simultaneously, both situations together at once. *One* situation is *both* situations. Both situations mean both romanticism and the threat from foreign territory. In romantic situations usually you're settling down, helping yourself to something, lying back and enjoying the pleasure. That's romanticism. And foreign territory means being up in arms, watchful.

The Trungpas had the same experience as the pioneering Kagyüpas. In some sense, it was on a much lesser scale than Milarepa, Marpa, and Naropa, but the Trungpas had a similar kind of experience constantly taking place. One of the Kagyü mystics once said, "Being in the Kagyü tradition, the Kagyü lineage, is like inheriting constant mishaps." Constant mishaps. That's true. If you are actually in contact with reality, and particularly if you are in control of reality, then you are in contact with completely constant mishaps. Because you are in contact and in control, therefore the mishaps begin to come to you rather than you bumping into them. They begin to come to you constantly. These little things are taking place all the time. Fantastic. Delightful. And it is that which makes everything very cheerful.

Take the story of Milarepa. He was told by Marpa that he could leave his guru and go back to his home. He had finally been accepted by Marpa, who had made him his chief disciple and an important person, the only son of the lineage. Milarepa was completely fine, feeling extremely good. Then he went back to his family home and everything was ruined, completely destroyed. That kind of mishap is always apropos of the Practicing Lineage, once you begin to have any association with the lineage. Milarepa found his house ruined, his mother enskeletoned inside. Nobody had even conducted a funeral service for her. His father was long dead, and his aunt and uncle and everybody were up in arms and there were no friends—none at all. It was like returning to a completely haunted house, like the haunted house in Disneyland. Everything is seemingly shrieking and haunting. Of course, for Milarepa this was not regarded as a ride, like in Disneyland. In Milarepa's case it was real.

One shrieking situation after another shrieking situation, one haunted situation after another haunted situation takes place because you are on top of situations. We would like to come face-to-face with a ghost. We hear stories about ghosts, and we would like to find out whether ghosts actually exist or not. If you are in a playful mood, ghosts don't appear, because they are not interested in haunting you at that point. Ghosts are only interested in haunting you when you are in a transitional period or else when you are on top of the situation. On the other hand, we are not talking about the reality of ghosts here. We don't want to get back into that psychic phenomenal world. That's another waste of time, of course. But ghosts will come to us. They come to you. [*Laughter*]

The Practicing Lineage is very much in contact with what's going on, virtually what is going on, actually what is going on, on the spot, on the dot, constantly. Interestingly, students in the Kagyü tradition have had less guidance from substantial phenomena, or the realistic world. In other words, they had less tutorship from people telling them how to do things or how not to do them. They had to take chances all the time, constantly. But they have more commitment to their guru, their teacher. So they have more devotion at the same time, which is an interesting point. When you have completely signed on with a church or an existing club, the company pays for the damage. Or else you are completely abandoned. Between those situations, there is some sense of actual reality taking place. How much you are connected with reality somewhat depends on your degree of sanity. At the same time, your disconnection with reality also comes through—a message will come through very clearly, strongly, properly.

Before we get into too many details about the line of the Trungpas, I would like to lay the ground for you so that you understand the difference between the Practicing Lineage and other lineages. So I will be interested in further feedback, such as your nightmares, your dreams, your thoughts about the whole thing.

Allen Ginsberg: Coming to you interested in Buddhism, what we wind up with is *you*, in a sense, or with your particular specialty, rather than some larger, maybe more vague Buddhism. But really, then, it comes right down to yourself and your lineage—which is often a kind of nightmare. [*Laughter*] Is that the way it's supposed to be?

Chögyam Trungpa Rinpoche: That's good. That's great. I'm sure that if you exchanged notes with Milarepa, he would say the same thing about his father, too. Maybe much more so.

AG: If this is the Practicing Lineage, do other lineages not practice as much?

CTR: Well, they do practice.

AG: What is the custom in the other lineages?

CTR: They do practice, but in many cases they don't *actually* practice. Very few people lock themselves in a cave. Nobody actually faces reality that far. Therefore this tradition is sometimes looked upon by other people as an evangelical tradition. The evangelical traditions of Christianity are slightly different, by the way. But getting off on the mountains, rocks, and caves, and locking yourself back in a cave and sitting a lot and devotioning a lot are regarded by some Buddhist lineages as an evangelical trip. We are definitely regarded as very eccentric. [*Laughter*]

Student: You talked about conquering the mountain and expanding. Aggression normally goes into conquering, expanding. Would you comment on that?

CTR: It's not so much aggression; it's more a sense of inspiration. If you are really hungry, you have a fantastic relationship with food. Let's say it's a hot dog. For many days, you want to have a hot dog. And finally you have a hot dog. You can actually have it on your paper dish, or whatever dish you have. You have a fantastic relationship with the hot dog. You eat it with complete delight and complete communication. That could be said to be a very aggressive trip. But I don't think that's true, actually, because you have open-mindedness toward that particular hot dog. You have designed visualizations and devotions [*laughter*] and you have a sense of longing, and everything's completely softened. You become softened, a soft person and a reasonable person. You have a hot dog, and you can eat that hot dog very beautifully, you know. You hold it in your hand and you feel it. You take a bite, and you chew it and feel the goodness of it at the same time. So it's a very real experience. That seems to be the difference between conquering, or expanding, and aggression, which is, you know, just completely off the wall. [*Prolonged laughter*]

S: In the same context, yesterday you referred to the distinction between desire and just making yourself available. When you're filled with neurotic desire to eat the hot dog, what do you do with that desire while you're waiting for the enlightened inspiration to be available?

CTR: That's a very difficult one, actually. Sometimes the desire can only be transmuted once you have what you desire. You can't have completely pure intention at the beginning. Your desire to have a hot dog in a neurotic fashion probably could wear off. When you begin to see that the actual hot dog is available, it begins to go beyond the realm of your imagination. There's actually a hot dog stand, and you can eat the hot dog, and your imagination doesn't have any role to play anymore. You're actually relating with an earthy situation. You see, we can't start perfectly, but once we begin to have any physical contact with a situation of that nature, then it can be worked out. So I wouldn't try to start with a transcendental hot dog. That would be deadly. Then you don't actually eat the hot dog at all. You think you are chewing some cosmic energy, swallowing the cosmic energy of the hot dog. You get entirely different results. You get high on eating the hot dog, and after that you begin to compose paeans and songs and you try to dance in celebration of the divineness of the hot dog—which is not necessary. Hot dog is hot dog. [*Laughter*] You could flush it down the toilet.

S: I'm not sure that I understood what you meant by inheriting constant mishaps, or that if you're on top of situations, the mishaps automatically come to you, if you know what's going on. Is that because what is always going on is actually a mishap?

CTR: If you know what's going on, that is a mishap? Did you say that? *No.* Something unexpected happens to you. When you find yourself being too naive, something else happens. In dictionary language, that's definitely a mishap. A mishap is a surprise. While trying to polish the table, you get a splinter in your finger. Something like that. A mishap is very, very understandable. It happens unexpectedly. That's why it's called "mishap," because it happens unexpectedly. You have been too naive, thinking that the smoothness of things will go on and everything's going to be OK. Suddenly something comes up—which is a mishap.

Let me tell you a little story. This happened recently. In the Buddhist community in Boulder, a couple decided to get married. His mother-in-law was terrified of driving on mountain roads. On the way to the wedding ceremony, the couple and the in-laws drove down from the mountains in two cars. Halfway down, the first car went off the mountain road and rolled over. Everything was OK. Nothing was broken. The people in the car crawled out of the windows, and they got in the other car and finished driving down, and everything was OK. They had the wedding ceremony. After the ceremony, they went back to the car to go to the reception, and they had two punctured tires. But everything went OK. That's the kind of mishap we're talking about, on a very small scale.

When you think that everything's going to be OK and everything's going to be fine, there are always reminders taking place. A larger degree would be Milarepa's mishap. Finally he was accepted by Marpa, who made him his chief disciple and an important person, the only son of the lineage. Milarepa felt extremely good. He went back home and everything was ruined. The whole place was completely destroyed. That kind of mishap is always apropos of our particular practicing lineage, once you begin to have any association with this kind of thing. Do you have more to say?

S: Was it Milarepa's fault that he found his home ruined and all of that?
CTR: Well, it's part of his creation. I wouldn't say it was his fault.
S: Was it a result of his lack of mindfulness or clumsiness? I have the impression that the reason the mishap is unexpected is because of some gap in a person's awareness.
CTR: What usually happens is that when you begin to relax in the teachings, but you are not quite adult enough, you're not grown up enough, at that point you're still thinking that everything is going to be OK. At that level, when the relaxation and the tension both begin to take place together, you get a mishap. Otherwise, how can you have the accident? An accident happens when tension and relaxation are put together.
S: So it's not anything as simple as lack of mindfulness.
CTR: That seems to be a layman's joke, you know, that you are not aware of yourself, so that is why something happened: "Look what you've done." It's like dealing with the kids, something like that. But in this case, it's actually much more sophisticated.
S: What is the element of tension?
CTR: Well, it's beyond nervousness. Rather than getting off, it's getting beyond. Having achieved something to get beyond the nervousness, there is an element of tension at the same time. It's like hot and cold air together creating explosions.
S: It seems as though you are saying that it's kind of a product of extra confidence, or something like that.
CTR: Well, at an introverted level it's a product of extra confidence. At the same time it's the product of extraordinary . . . distrustfulness, put together.
S: Where does the distrustfulness come in?
CTR: It comes from the fickleness of your uncertainty.

S: When you speak of being on top of the situation, that sounds like something positive. Yet you don't really mean being in contact with the situation.

CTR: When you are more in contact with a situation, you begin to get hit with both sides of the fever, so to speak. So you're more vulnerable.

S: Could there be a situation where nothing unexpected could happen to a person? Where mishaps couldn't occur because the person was so enlightened?

CTR: Sure, absolutely, there's the possibility of that. Let's not talk about that too much. That creates a further accident, if you talk too much about that. [*Laughter*]

CHAPTER THREE

Trung Ma-se and the Three Idiots

ONTINUING THE DISCUSSION of the Mishap Lineage, I would like to discuss further how practitioners develop as the product of such a tradition and discipline. Students become very realistic, earthbound, and ordinary, and at the same time highly awake, because no preconception exists within them. Their minds are completely set or attuned to the practice; therefore their understanding of the teachings becomes much clearer and more realistic.

Sometimes you interrupt your state of mind. You are continually concerned about the state of your sanity and concerned about how many preconceptions you are laying on your world or yourself. You question whether your ideas are too heavy or too light. Throughout that questioning process, even though the motivation and the situation may be right for practice and even though your understanding may be correct, at the same time those preconceptions begin to drive you into complete madness. You want to split hairs. You want to question the question of the question of the question of the question, constantly, again and again *and* again. In that case, you don't find any room to actually allow yourself to practice and sit and develop discipline at all.

In that situation, it is necessary to cultivate the students' simplemindedness. In some sense, we could say uneducatedness, not having too much of a sophisticated vocabulary, might be necessary in that situation. At the same time, the earthbound quality provides a lot of room or space to understand the teachings to the fullest, very precisely, very directly, on a real, direct, and straightforward level.

In the Practicing Lineage, when devotion is emphasized, it becomes natural devotion, direct devotion, earthbound devotion, as opposed to being equated with the father principle, mother principle, husband principle, or wife principle. Devotion is based on one's loneliness and one's claustrophobia. In that way, devotion becomes strict and direct at the same time. Whatever situations occur within the learning process, they become straightforward, rather than being looked at from too many angles with too much analytical process. Things are approached from a realistic level rather than just from the level of preconceptions. That provides the general atmosphere and the general approach to working with situations or the teachings, which is very up-to-date and applicable to the present, as much as it happened and was up-to-date in the past.

The Surmang lineage, which is the lineage of the Trungpas, began around the fifteenth century in Tibet. A child, Trung Ma-se, was born in the far east of Tibet in the principality of Minyak, a province that is now part of Szechuan. He was the son of a local lord from a family named Ma-se. This child happened to be illegitimate, and he was the youngest child in the family. There was some resentment of him because he was illegitimate, but still the family paid him a certain amount of respect, honoring him simply because he was born into this particular family. That particular area of Tibet was predominantly Nyingma, which as we discussed is the earliest school of Tibetan Buddhism. In school, students were taught the culture and the meditative traditions of the Nyingma school. When this child grew to be about fifteen, he became a very learned and powerful person of this particular principality.

His full name was Trung Ma-se. *Trung* is a classical term in Tibetan for an attendant to the guru. *Trung* means "closest to the teacher." So *Ma-se* was the family name and *Trung* referred to somebody who was the closest to his guru, which in Trung Ma-se's case was the Fifth Karmapa, Teshin Shekpa.

The birthplace of Trung Ma-se was in what would become the province of Surmang, which is where the Trungpa lineage was established a little later. The king of Minyak was making a pilgrimage to Lhasa, and Trung

Ma-se's mother was part of the traveling party. This illegitimate child was born in the same area where the Surmang monasteries would be established in the future. When I was at Surmang, there was a particular place, a certain field, which we referred to as the place where the king of Minyak had set up his encampment. It was there in that particular place that this child was born. [Presumably, the king then returned to Minyak, where Trung Ma-se was raised.—Ed.]

The child was raised in both the spiritual and the temporal, or secular, disciplines that had evolved at that time. When he was older, he wanted to leave his homeland [Minyak], and he did so with the permission of his parents. He journeyed to Central Tibet. He had already received the teachings of the *ati* tradition from the Nyingma school as part of his upbringing. In Central Tibet, he visited the Fifth Karmapa, Teshin Shekpa, and received instruction from the Karmapa. He remained there practicing for something like seven years.

The Karmapa encouraged Trung Ma-se to return to East Tibet and to establish himself there, in a certain place [that turned out to be close to where he was born]. Following the Karmapa's instructions, Trung Ma-se went to a geographical location where he established a monastic retreat hut and began to teach a group of students. The province that he went to at that time was controlled by a local lord who was called Adro Shelu-bum. *Adro* was the family name and *Shelu-bum* was the first name. Under his leadership, there were something like nine hundred families in an area comprising perhaps three hundred square miles of property. There was a lot of timberland, and also a lot of highlands with a great pasture area and a salt lake. This is where Ma-se established his hermitage.[1]

His dwelling place was a reed hut. Having practiced and taught there for quite a long time, Trung Ma-se began to attract many prominent students. Eventually, he was teaching to a public audience of several thousand students. Many hundreds of his devotees, something like three hundred and sixty of them, were considered close students. Among these, there were eight very close students, who were known as the "eight mystics." Then there were the three idiots, who were the closest students of all. The First Trungpa was one of the idiots.

The reason they were known as idiots was because they were so stubborn and so earthy that they did not flinch at anything at all. They simply set their minds to one thing at a time. When the teacher told them to do something, they just did it. They became known as the idiots for their stubbornness. The eight mystics were quite good in their idiotness, but they didn't quite qualify to be known as idiots. They were somewhat good students and nice people.[2]

As Trung Ma-se's teaching situation became stronger and clearer, his students requested that he give a name to his establishment, saying, "We don't have a name for what we are doing here." Trung Ma-se suggested that they could name the establishment after his reed hut. It had a lot of corners, because a reed hut needs a lot of support, which is provided by all the corners. Therefore they called the place "Surmang." *Sur* means "corner" and *mang* means "many," so *Surmang* means "many cornered." It was quite arbitrary. He wasn't particularly concerned with creating a glorious name.[3]

Unfortunately, we have very little direct information about Trung Ma-se and his approach to spirituality. Some information can be abstracted from various teaching manuals about other subjects. There are very few stories about how Trung Ma-se actually conducted himself, but his story begins to come through in manuscripts and other places where there are stories about the Trungpas and also about the three idiots altogether. Seemingly, Trung Ma-se was very concerned with trying to blend together the Nyingma tradition and the Kagyü tradition. The Nyingma tradition was his inheritance in terms of his family background, while the Kagyü tradition was his inheritance from the teachings that he had received from the Fifth Karmapa.[4]

Trung Ma-se was known to be a very powerful person, but he was not a particularly metaphysically outspoken person, to say the least. He was married, and his plan was to continue the Trung family lineage through successive generations of priests. In Tibet in those days it often happened that lineages were continued through the family of the teacher. On the other hand, he also intended to have another lineage, which would be continued by a student carrying on the lineage through instruction to future generations. Somehow, Trung Ma-se's family lineage didn't continue.[5]

I think that his approach toward discipline was extraordinarily simple and straightforward. He always recommended sitting practice as the most important discipline. In those days, this was known as "devoting yourself to the caves." He also taught that it was important to have a sense of celebration at the same time. Beginning in those days, that sense of celebration became an important part of the Surmang tradition. People were constantly having feasts, and they received a sense of delight from their teacher and an appreciation for what was happening.

Toward the end of his life, Trung Ma-se didn't stay in the place where his reed hut was, but he traveled all around the province in a huge caravan, camping in different places. This caravan was known as the "caravan of joyousness." The villages that had famines and depressions, problems after problems, were waiting for the joyousness camp to arrive and cheer them up, so that a further sense of humor could develop. It seems that this concept of an encampment is still continuing in our situation, in some sense. Toward the end of Trung Ma-se's life, he traveled with the three idiots and the eight mystics and the three hundred and sixty close disciples altogether—he covered a lot of ground in that part of Tibet. A lot of people in that area began to regard Trung Ma-se as their teacher.

Trung Ma-se's approach to working with people was very mechanical in some sense, but on the other hand it was seeing situations clearly as a game, playing with situations. Trung Ma-se's approach was not so much to have a clear vision to begin with. His approach was first to take advantage of whatever arose in situations, and then clear vision would develop out of that. That seemed to be how the whole thing worked, and that has been continuously happening, up to this particular age.

Student: Rinpoche, what did you mean about working with situations and then clear vision developing, as opposed to having clear vision and then involvement with a situation? I'm not quite sure of the distinction.
Chögyam Trungpa Rinpoche: First there has to be a mishap. You remember? Then that *is* the situation. On top of the mishap, there is clear vision. You begin to evolve and involve yourself beyond the mishap, and you begin to expand beyond that particular situation. Any problems with that? Can you ask me more questions about that?
S: Well, we might say that the mishap was caused by not having clear vision to begin with.

CTR: Clear vision to begin with doesn't have any ground. It's just clear vision, which purely means concepts and chain reactions of some kind. We could use the establishment of our practice centers in America as an example. Take the example of Karmê Chöling, the first center in America. We had a mishap [that brought me and my students from England to America], which was based on chain reactions, and on that basis Karmê Chöling was founded by a group of people. Everything was operating on mistakes of all kinds. Then we began to use those mistakes as the ground to operate on, and then we began to correct the mistakes and evolve further. It's something like that. I don't have to go into too much detail particularly, testimonial-style.

S: You've been talking a lot about the Practicing Lineage in the last few days. Tonight you mentioned the emphasis in the Kagyü tradition on going to caves and that being something unique in the Kagyü tradition as opposed to other sects. We seem to be talking about something that took place six or seven hundred years ago. What is the real difference between the experience of someone like Milarepa or one of Trung Ma-se's students and our experience?

CTR: Not very much. I mean, the only difference is that they heard different noises then. These days we might hear airplanes flying above, and in those days they might hear flies buzzing about. Otherwise, it's pretty much the same. The American approach, in the USA, is thinking that ancient times were more romantic. Antiques are fantastic to Americans because this country is very young and doesn't have a lot of antiques. Americans have nostalgia about Europe or any *old* place where you can get old stuff. The prices are fantastic. Dealers make money on that. A lot of antiques are shipped to America these days. They send over anything that's old, including a little peg, an old mug, whatever they have.

In actual reality, as far as the living situation is concerned, it's essentially the same then and now. There's nothing very different. In those days caves were routinely used for sitting practice, not for romantic reasons but because in that geographical area, there were lots of caves. You didn't have to spend money to build a cabin; there were holes in the mountains already. You just went and lived there. But nowadays we can't find many holes in the mountains around here. It's simply a question of geography. So we have to build cabins. Then we have to meet with the inspectors about the health code, or whatever. Those are incidental issues. Basically, it's still the same thing. Actually things haven't changed that much.

This is an important point. We might romanticize the "good old days," but if you were there right now, you wouldn't think that these were the "good old days" at all. You would have the same experience then as now, anyway. It's just a gap in time, a time lapse. But it was the same then as what we are doing right now.

S: Rinpoche, how is Trung Ma-se's technique a blend of the Nyingma tradition and the Kagyü? How is it different than either one separately?
CTR: It's not particularly different, but it's very clever, in some sense. The Nyingma tradition was his heritage. He was brought up that way from childhood. He didn't regard the Kagyü tradition as stepping out of his own background into another tradition. Instead, he found that he was able to blend the whole thing together.

In this country, problems may exist. When somebody studies with more than one teacher, even if both teachers are from the same lineage, the student may find it difficult to blend the whole thing together. That is a problem inherited from the Christian tradition, which is to say it's a guilt complex. Trung Ma-se never heard of Christ. That might sound like a terrible thing to say, very shocking and completely heathen. However, he was a complete human being, if I may say so, a pure human being who could actually relate with reality. The inheritance from his family and the inheritance from his lineage could be brought together without any problems.
S: It was more just his experience of the teachings?
CTR: Yes, the sameness of it. The beauty of both could be put together. It is like a jewel mounted in gold. Something like that. Sunshine in the sky. Very simple.

S: Rinpoche, yesterday when you spoke about mishaps, I had the feeling that this was almost like a technique or a tool that the Kagyü used to create a sort of in-between space of transition where things could happen. Today, you are speaking of mishaps as being just a series of circumstances, coincidences, perhaps. Is the mishap both of those things, or is it—?

CTR: I think I would say both, considering present situations. Both.

S: What present situation?

CTR: Your guess is as good as mine. *The* present situation. [*Laughter*]

S: Rinpoche, what kinds of things did Trung Ma-se do to form a relationship with so many students? How was he able to do that in so short a period of time?

CTR: Well, he was dealing with the three idiots. Remember those? And the eight mystics and the rest of them. He didn't have to particularly relate with every one of those students too much, manually, but he began to develop some kind of sangha-ship. *Sangha*—do you understand that word?

S: No, but I was waiting for you to pause before I asked.

CTR: It is group spirit and group sanity, which is transmitted *through*, constantly. Then things don't have to get caught in a bottleneck situation anymore. Group spirit, group sanity: the Kagyü tradition works with that always. And that's what we are doing here, too. Group sanity. Group sanity as opposed to group encounter. [*Laughter*]

S: As opposed to groupie?

CTR: Yes. Allen?

Allen Ginsberg: What is the Tibetan etymology for *idiots* and *mystics*? Was that a structural tradition that came through the Trungpa line?

CTR: Well, the Tibetan word for "idiot" is *ja* (Tib. *ja 'mo*).[6] It's a very localized idiom, which literally means "moron." [*Laughter*]

AG: Literally?

CTR: Literally, it's the three morons. *Ja* actually means "lower, flat, and very naive-like," like a sitting duck. [*Laughter*] The word for "mystics" is *tobden* (Tib. *rtogs ldan*), which means "someone who is realized" or "endowed with realization."

AG: Did those categories continue? Were they repeated in the Trungpa line, or was it just that one occasion?

CTR: It was just that one occasion. We didn't have any further idiots. [*Laughter*] I beg your pardon!
AG: I was hoping to be an idiot. [*Laughs; laughter*]

S: The notion of the sitting duck brings up the idea of mishaps, too. I mean, it's just waiting—
CTR: Definitely so.

S: Last night in your description of mishap, you mentioned a number of elements. You described a combination of relaxation and tension. Under tension, you said that one of the elements was distrustfulness. And you said that was fickleness about one's own uncertainty. Could you talk more about this fickleness? I have a feeling for it, but I'm not quite clear just what that is.
CTR: I think that uncertainty comes from jumping back and forth, rather than solid uncertainty taking place. You see what I mean? Uncertainty is never really solid. It's jumping back and forth.
S: Between certainty and uncertainty?
CTR: Yes.
S: Is it conceivable that one could arrive at a state of solid uncertainty? Could you sit down and really think about it for a while?
CTR: No, not at all. Then it couldn't be uncertainty.
S: It would become—
CTR: It would become very certain, very real. Yes or no. [*Grinds his teeth*] There's no fickleness when you have a [*grinds teeth ferociously; laughter*]. It's all set in the gothic style.

Language is interesting. *Uncertain:* not having certainty. *Uncertain*, meaning not *quite* certain, but still it is certain in some sense. So there's lots of room to move back and forth. It's like the word *unknown*, which doesn't mean *completely* without knowledge. It implies there are possibilities of knowing and possibilities of not knowing. Therefore, something is "unknown." It's just behind the curtain, behind the venetian blind. There could be lots of possibilities of that, at the same time.

S: What are we poor souls, who have a whole bunch of ideas already, to do?

CTR: To begin with, you don't have souls. [*Laughter*] And your ideas are not solid ideas, because they are not founded on aggression or dogma. You have open ideas, which we work with all the time, anyway. There is no problem with that. Ideas are not founded on solid ground. They are just . . . ideas. That's a very important point, actually. Can you say something more about that?

S: I feel that I have so many ideas about what should happen or what I want to happen or how you should be or how the teachings should be. So I don't feel open and receptive to what is really happening.

CTR: That seems to be good, actually, utterly good. That particular open-and-closed fickleness tends to bring a lot of understanding. Whereas if you completely buy in, so to speak, then it's like being caught in the jaws of a crocodile. You have no outside reference point. You are just completely buying in. That seems to be one of the problems with many present spiritual advertisements. It's like the Divine Light approach: either you are *in it* or you are not in it.[7] Out . . . in. You can't actually experience the space between the two. That is a problem, and that seems to be a spiritual materialistic trick to use on people: trying to save them from their problems. I think that approach is based on a hesitation or inability to provide everything legitimately, step-by-step. The leaders of a trip feel somewhat inadequate, so they tell potential students, "Buy it or don't buy it." That seems to be too cheap.

S: So is it best to have a questioning attitude?

CTR: Yes, absolutely. Spiritual discipline is not based on becoming somebody else. But you become you—in your enlightened version. That is the whole point.

S: Is this fickleness and uncertainty supposed to characterize vajrayana study too?

CTR: Yep—but on a much more . . . suicidal level.

S: Is it a suicidal contest with the teacher?

CTR: With yourself. However, that level of understanding and practice is beyond what we're discussing.

CHAPTER FOUR

Tent Culture

I WOULD LIKE TO discuss the experience of establishing monasticism, at the beginner's level of starting an administration as well as discussing the continuing potential chain reactions of an organization. As far as Trung Ma-se was concerned, he was quite nonchalant about the outcome of working with particular students. However, he paid attention to *how* the administration would work, and how in the future people would reflect back on the situation and work with the projects he had started.

One concern seemed to be future problems: how the teachings might deteriorate or be diluted or misguided in the future. In order to save us from such problems, how could his particular presentation be made more lively and be more powerfully presented? As far as Trung Ma-se was concerned, his approach to presenting the dharma was taking care of both situations at once: the present situation and the future. He emphasized that people should respect their personal practice, the sitting practice of meditation, and the training that they were going through. However, he didn't give any particular administrative guidelines or set up anything at all for the future. Everything was purely presented in a homemade fashion, based on human connections alone.

From the establishment of those types of human connections, a lot of students began to erupt into emotionality, complaints, and uncertainties of all kinds. Those things were accepted as part of the journey. The teaching situation was not purely based on political manipulation or on a political visionary level alone. It was very personal. Students got freaked out, students got depressed, and they felt unworthy. Sometimes they felt that they could do better; they felt that they could do something else with their lives, so they would leave and take a trip around the countryside. At the same time, there was the basic genuineness of their individual dedication. In those days, people living in the Surmang area and in the area around Adro Shelu-bum's lands were so fascinated by the teachings—as much as people are fascinated by the teachings today on this continent. They felt that there was a great deal that they wanted to learn, study, and practice with this particular teacher, Trung Ma-se. At the same time, the situation was mysterious . . . much like what is taking place here in this country.

The First Trungpa was Kunga Gyaltsen, which literally means "All Joyful Victory Banner." He was born and raised as an aristocrat, a prince, in a neighboring principality. Growing up, he was fully educated in reading, writing, and arithmetic. He received a complete basic training, based on what the tradition allowed. Then he went to study with Trung Ma-se. Having studied with him and become one of the idiots, he returned to his home area, where he practiced in a jungle of neem trees. The twigs and bark from the neem tree are used for brushing your teeth, and the plant has many other medicinal properties. Kunga Gyaltsen sat and practiced in a grove of neem trees for something like ten years. In addition to the sitting practice of meditation, he practiced all kinds of yogic disciplines. After many years, he was urged by his teacher, Trung Ma-se, to take a trip around the neighborhood.[1]

Kunga Gyaltsen had a dream, which told him that in order to establish the ground for his future monastery, he should acknowledge himself as an incarnation of the Indian saint Dombipa. He should throw a cup of *chang* in the air, which is a Tibetan beer made out of barley. The cup would fly through the air and wherever it landed, that particular spot would be the future location of his monastery, his establishment.

When he woke up from this dream, the First Trungpa was somewhat concerned as to whether this dream was purely of his own making or if something more was taking place. Making predictions from dreams, or dream yoga, was regarded with suspicion in those days, which is always true in the Buddhist tradition. Dream practice or dream predictions are regarded as phantoms. Sometimes they somehow make sense, particularly if your state of mind is in the right frame of reference. Then dreams are regarded as a worthwhile thing to relate with. But otherwise, dreams are regarded as purely neurotic garbage.

In this case, Kunga Gyaltsen, the First Trungpa, decided to follow the inspiration that came out of his dream. He had a cup full of beer, and he decided to throw it up in the air.[2] It flew beyond his visual perception. Supposedly there was a big explosion of some kind, a big bang, when the cup landed. It actually landed on the rooftop of Adro Shelu-bum's second palace, which is now called *Dütsi Tel*, which means "Hill of Amrita" (*amrita* means "blessed liquor"). News went all over the country that due to some miraculous power, an object had landed on the flat rooftop of Adro Shelu-bum's abode. Adro Shelu-bum and his court and his subjects were all concerned as to whether this was a bad omen or a good omen.

This gossip got back to the First Trungpa, so he decided to walk over to Adro Shelu-bum's palace and find out what happened. While he was walking there, Kunga Gyaltsen was reciting a text of Manjushri. When he reached the doorstep of the palace, he came to a particular line in the sutra, which says, "Firmly plant the victorious banner of dharma."[3] He repeated that line three times. At our monastery, Surmang Dütsi Tel, we repeat that particular line twice when we chant the sutra. Currently, that line has been made into one of the main phrases, or slogans, of Naropa University.[4] We have translated it as "We firmly plant the banner of victory of dharma." That has become the logo, the expression or motto, shall we say, of Naropa University.

When Kunga Gyaltsen arrived at the palace of Adro Shelu-bum, he found his cup there. He approached Lord Adro and identified the cup as his. He described certain cracks and scratches on his cup, which was actually a wooden bowl.[5] It definitely was his own cup. Adro Shelu-bum's people checked and they verified what the First Trungpa had described. So Adro Shelu-bum was extraordinarily impressed by this. Lord Adro was a very courteous, kind, and very religious person. He decided to offer as much hospitality as he could to Kunga Gyaltsen, and to accommodate him by providing the right kind of teaching situation for him. Kunga Gyaltsen at that point accepted the hospitality and the acknowledgment from the lord of the principality. He accepted the offer to use Adro Shelu-bum's palace to teach his disciples, his students, during a certain portion of the year. However, they didn't want to be pinned down by establishing a monastery. He and his students wanted to be free to travel around.

It's an interesting point that the First Trungpa had hesitation about establishing anything, any institution, completely. Also, he had a longing to firmly plant the seed of dharma in society. That is somewhat a dubious situation, somewhat schizophrenic, we could say. We can use that word positively. There's no problem with that. He wanted to be loose; at the same time, he wanted to create something permanent. A lot of traditions have begun that way, particularly within the Kagyü lineage. For instance, Milarepa didn't want to call what he was doing the Practitioner's Lineage, particularly. Then at the time of Gampopa, it became known as the "Practitioner's Lineage" or the "Practicing Lineage of the Kagyü." So that's an interesting reference point from an earlier time.

In the time of the First Trungpa, there were very few solid, permanent monastic situations established. Particularly, a lot of the Kagyüpas didn't want to settle down in one place, and they traveled in large encampments, or caravans. This included the Karmapas, up to the seventh or even the eighth generation of Karmapas. For instance, there is a story about the drum used by the Fifth Karmapa and his party. They had a huge drum that was used in many ceremonies. The drum could be taken apart in sections and loaded onto a mule pack, or a yak pack, whatever they had. Whenever they encamped, the drum could be put back together, and the skin could be stretched overnight.

Everything was adapted for a traveling group situation, which was somewhat based on ideas borrowed from Genghis Khan and Mongolian culture all together. It was possible to set up a magnificent capital, a temporary modern city, right on the spot. They set up residence tents as well as the main meditation hall where ceremonies were conducted and abhishekas were performed. Then the next day, they would pack up the whole thing and move on.

Apart from the Romans, in the West we find very little tent culture. The Tibetan tent culture, however, was prominent and became powerfully important. There are some theories that this tent culture actually influenced the Chinese court and the Chinese military culture. At that time, all of the Kagyü traditions developed what was known as a *gar*, which is the Tibetan word for "encampment." Interestingly, this provided possibilities of establishing complete splendor in one night. The next day, the whole thing could be disassembled and the people could continue on their journey. That tradition is extraordinarily powerful and wondrous at the same time for a lot of people.

The age of encampment extended from the fourteenth century into the late sixteenth century, as far as Tibetan monasticism goes. The camps were constantly moving. It was a much more grandiose level than gypsies and much more powerful than military camps. Villagers would wake up in the morning and go out to take their herds into the mountains. They would look down into the next valley and find a whole huge monastery encamped there. It's a fantastic concept. The villagers would be hoping that the camp would be there for a long time. Then the next day when they woke up, the camp was gone. All that was left were the rocks that were used in the stoves. Or there might be little dying fires, horse dung, mule dung, or whatever.

That type of monastery was able to travel to a lot of areas. Each time the camp arrived somewhere, they could give the local people a real demonstration of their understanding of how to conduct an administration and how to conduct ceremonies properly. It's like Karmê Chöling, which is a rural practice center, coming to New York, Karmê Chöling going to Boston, Karmê Chöling being in Ottawa or Texas. Each day in each place, you could see full-fledged, real monasticism actually taking place . . . quite free from those little caravan trips of Steve Gaskin or whoever you have.[6]

In this case, the real thing was actually taking place. The full splendor, wealth, and dignity was manifested. Sometimes hippies make a big deal about camping out. I don't know whether it's actually hippies or beatniks—I'm not sure—but for such people, traveling in a caravan is regarded as a fantastic thing to do. They are promoting funkiness at the same time, rather than the establishment of such *splendor* and such magnificent tents.

According to the stories of the Karmapa's camps, the huge assembly tent came in seventy-five parts. Each part was loaded onto a mule. When they made camp, they would assemble the whole tent and button it together. It was a huge assembly hall, with magnificent brocades hanging in it, *thangkas* everywhere and fantastic rugs on the floor. There were magnificent thrones and seats for people to sit on and do their practice. The shrine was fully assembled. This was far from any kind of hippie trip or beatnik trip, if I may say so. It was *real*, doing the whole thing 100 percent.

It's an interesting point that we haven't developed that kind of tent culture in America at all. The way to reduce pollution and save ourselves from urbanization might be to have a fantastic magnificent dharma tent culture. You could establish the whole situation at once, on the spot, with all its splendor. The organization could fulfill its duties wherever it goes. The administration would have a chance to relate with each locality as well, and then fold everything up and move somewhere else. That is a very heroic and very Buddhistic approach: nothing is particularly permanent, but you keep on moving all the time.

That's what the First Trungpa did. He developed the first Surmang Garchen, which means the "great camp of the Surmang people."[7] It turned out to be very successful. It was a fantastic display of how you can actually handle life, not leaving too much mess except for the little dying fires that you leave behind when you break camp. Little areas of grass have been burnt because you set fire to them in order to put a kitchen there. The rest of the field stayed pretty neat.

In those days, Tibetans were very involved with tent culture. We could say that we are still involved with tent culture somewhat. Hopefully, ours won't be too much like caravan parks, trailer parks where you have your own little house, electricity, and toilet system. In that situation, you can't actually move; you're fastened to your ground. Modern tent culture also shouldn't be a hippie trip or a beatnik trip at all. It should be a genuine, dignified situation.

In the time of the First Trungpa, there was tremendous appreciation of the Surmang camp throughout the locality, or the neighborhood. The camp was set up in the highlands in the summertime, where they could enjoy the yogurt, milk, and cheese of the highlanders. In the autumn and the wintertime, the camp moved down to the lowlands to enjoy the grain and vegetables of the lowlanders.

This was a work of immense vision. These people were quite aware that eventually they would have to settle down in one particular place. At the same time, they were interested in and open to the tent culture of Tibet of that particular age, that time in history.

Student: I'm not quite sure I understand why there was such a need for an elaborate tent culture, which seems a bit of a contradiction to the simplicity of the picture you described before. How could people separate out the materialism when they saw such a magnificent array?

Chögyam Trungpa Rinpoche: People at the time were confused. I wouldn't say that the whole thing was perfectly ideal, actually. You should take it with a pinch of salt—the whole thing. Spiritual materialism could be taking place, obviously. But at the same time, the teachers were trying to communicate, reach out, with the message of dharma to everyone, very simply. I'm sure that the splendor and the royalty did come out of spiritual materialism, obviously. That always happens.

One of the interesting points is that problems of spiritual materialism are more prominent these days in the West. In those days, people did not have the automation of machines and drugs of all kinds—downers and uppers. In those days, people felt that they could still take their time going through things. But these days, particularly in the United States and in North America in general, there are lots of drugs, lots of machines, and lots of quick promises. Charlatans are available to keep you from any hard way of working with situations.

In those days people had less time to use tricks. Everything was manual. If you had to put up a tent, it took a lot of time to do that. If you wanted to move camp, that involved a journey. Everything was very manual, all the time. Nothing was automated. If you were tired or sick, you couldn't reach anybody by calling them up on the telephone, saying, "Save me!" You couldn't take a taxi. Everything had to be done manually. Unavailability of that kind is very, very powerful. The manual world saves sanity.

S: Is there some connection between a particular monastic tradition settling down in one place and the idea of lineage, such as the lineage of the Karmapas or the lineage of the Trungpas?

CTR: Probably there is. I don't know exactly what to say about that. I think both apply. An encampment is powerful, and at the same time having a solid situation is also very powerful.

S: It seemed that the line of the Trungpas started when the First Trungpa settled down in one spot, and the line of the Karmapas started when Gampopa established a monastic situation. Is there a direct connection between a monastic situation developing and the rest of the lineage becoming an ongoing thing as well?

CTR: I think so. There's some truth in that. Let's wait and see what happens here in America.

S: Could you say a little bit more about the Indian saint that Kunga Gyaltsen dreamed about?

CTR: Dombipa? Can you say something, Robin? [Speaking to one of his students, Robin Kornman.—Ed.]

Robin Kornman: Actually not. I don't know much about Dombipa.

CTR: I'm sure you can. Get the microphone.

RK: I have to put my ignorance on tape?

CTR: Yes. [*Laughter*]

RK: December 23, 1975. I don't remember anything about Dombipa. [*Laughter*]

CTR: Anybody else? OK. Wait for the microphone so that you can be taped.

S: As I recall, Dombipa was an Indian *siddha* who at some point in his life had a skull cup, and he said, "I'm going to throw this skull cup in the air and, many generations in the future, I'll be reincarnated where this skull cup lands." He threw it in the air in India, and it flew to where the Surmang monasteries were later established in Tibet.

CTR: Yes. Dombipa was born as a Brahman, very high class, in India. The Trungpas are a reincarnation of Dombipa. He was raised in a Brahman household, and he studied Buddhism. He was a student of *mahamudra*. In those days, Buddhism—tantra as well as mahayana and hinayana—flourished in India.

As far as his parents were concerned, a fatal moment in Dombipa's life occurred when, although he was a Brahman, he took a girl from a lower caste, an untouchable, as his girlfriend, his consort. This shocked his parents immensely. Not only that, but he went up to the rooftop of his parents' house, and he was constantly partying up there with this girl, drinking and making love all the time. That was happening simultaneously, all the time. Finally his parents got very upset, thinking that he was going to ruin their reputation as a good Brahman family. The father was also some kind of local chieftain, and this behavior would misrepresent their social placement.

Dombipa would drink something like seven gallons of Indian alcohol in one night. I don't know what it's called. In Tibet, we would call this drink *chang*. He was having a good time on the rooftop drinking and being with his girlfriend. He was already an accomplished siddha, an accomplished meditator, a realized person, so he knew what he was doing. But his parents didn't. Usually, that's the case. [*Laughter*] There's a saying that the first people to know you are your parents, and you are the last people they know. First and last. So they have difficulties, obviously. They were worried about the respectability of Dombipa's social situation. In fact, his family name wasn't Dombipa. *Dombipa* means "he who relates with the lower caste."

One day his father and mother got very upset, and they decided to climb up on the rooftop. Before, they were too horrified to even go up there and do anything about what was happening. Finally, the whole thing became too much for them. So they went up on the rooftop, and they were going to arrest the couple and have both of them put in jail. Dombipa, realizing what they were up to, kicked over seven gallons of liquor with one blow, and he flew up in the air, levitating with his consort. Those seven gallons became much more than seven. Liquor was churning out of the container, an unending stream of liquor. It flooded the whole house and then the whole village. Everybody was about to drown. The parents had run away, but they came back to the rooftop and supplicated Dombipa, saying, "Please forgive us." Then Dombipa sang a famous song, which was translated into Tibetan later. He sang, "He who knows the nature of mind, does not know the nature of confusion,"[8] and so forth. Then his parents and the whole village were converted to Buddhism. [*Laughter*]

Then Dombipa left the palace with this lower-caste, supposedly terrible dirty woman, and he rode on a tiger. Occasionally people would see him riding his tiger here and there in the jungle. He finally became a real siddha.

Supposedly, he appeared to be constantly drunk, as well as riding on a tiger at the same time. [*Laughter*]

S: I wonder if you could say something about the nature of Buddhism in Tibet at the time of the First Trungpa. Hadn't Buddhism been established in Tibet for many centuries? Why was it necessary for the Trungpas to be doing all this tent traveling?

CTR: Buddhism wasn't properly established at all. There were just dots, patches, at that time.

S: So the people were still practicing the Bön tradition?

CTR: Yes. You see, Tibetans are very dense. The population was not all that big, but people were very dense, very stubborn. Individually they were very powerful people. In order to get through to one person, it would take much more than Billy Graham can imagine. [*Laughter*] There was no room for mass conversion. People had to be dealt with individually, somewhat, which we as Tibetans are proud of. I don't think Tibetans would be willing to buy televisions or radios, particularly. They would like to talk to the newscaster personally. [*Laughter*]

I would like to encourage you to practice as much as you can. You might find yourself hesitating, thinking you're unable to do so, which is completely regarded as bullshit, or more likely as monkey shit. [*Laughter*] You can do so. Please take part in the sitting practice of meditation as much as you can, in the name of the Trungpas personally and the rest of the lineage. Thank you.

CHAPTER FIVE

The Fourth Trungpa[1]

IN DISCUSSING FURTHER questions about the line of the Trungpas, there are a lot of interesting points. The First Trungpa established a starting point for administering and organizing the learning situation, the teaching situation, but that was not quite enough. Having started by sowing the seeds in the spring, how are we going to handle the rest of the year? The summer and the autumn still depend on us. Similarly, having founded a monastic institution by means of the tent culture we discussed, the tradition was still very dependent on the commitment of individuals. Practitioners began to sit a lot, much more so in those days than what we are doing here. And students began to learn and understand the philosophy behind the practice as well. The floating organization [the tent culture established by Kunga Gyaltsen] meant that no permanent establishment was provided. At the same time, wherever the camp moved, it encouraged the creation of a permanent establishment there, since they had to continuously set up an administrative center wherever the camp traveled.

After the time of Kunga Gyaltsen, the First Trungpa, the teaching situation continued through the reign of four generations of Trungpas. The tent culture was still continuing at the time of the Fourth Trungpa, Kunga Namgyal. At that point, the Surmang caravan had grown immensely, to such a great extent that there were now several thousand people involved. Many devotees were still joining the Surmang encampment.

In the reign of the Fourth Trungpa, Kunga Namgyal, he decided to turn the forts that had been offered to the Trungpas into permanent monastic situations. All the *dzongs*, which means "castles" or "forts," were made into monastic headquarters. They were no longer forts or castles. The big audience halls, assembly halls, and meeting halls were converted into meditation halls, and little rooms were converted into monks' living quarters, and so forth.

At that point, there was a sense of conquering the secular situation, a sense of victory over the secular situation that was already set up, and turning that environment into a spiritual situation. The monks and their abbots began to establish their monastic headquarters. Dütsi Tel, which was an extension of Adro Shelu-bum's original castle, as we discussed previously, was finally established as a permanent monastery.

The monastic setup became the central focus of society, much more so than before. Finally at that point, the principality, that particular kingdom around Surmang, began to hand over the administrative duties, as well as the spiritual duties, to the Trungpas. The Fourth Trungpa received acknowledgment from the Chinese emperor as an important political leader. He was presented with seals of all kinds from the emperor. In his youth he was horrified by his political role, unlike the rest of the Trungpas who came after his generation. He handed over the political administrative duties to his brother, who was then acknowledged by the emperor of China as being an important, powerful local ruler.

The Fourth Trungpa set off by himself, purely by himself. He acquired a hornless yak, which is a pack animal that is particularly trained for carrying a load. The yak's nose was punctured through, so that you could put a loop through it. Then wherever you needed to lead the yak, it would go with its master. That's a traditional practice in Tibet. The animal is called *nalo* (Tib. *sna lo*), which literally means the "looped-nose one." Packing his bags and his supplies onto this animal, the Fourth Trungpa set forth to visit 108 pilgrimage places around the neighborhood. According to folktales, a lot of these places were supposedly completely haunted by ghosts of all kinds. He also meditated in the caves a great deal. His whole journey took about three years.

At the end of the third year, Kunga Namgyal came back to his monastery after he had accomplished his visit around the countryside. Immediately he went into retreat for six years, about a half mile from Dütsi Tel Monastery of Surmang. He did his retreat in a cave that is presently a retreat center. If you look at the drawings in *Born in Tibet*, there is an architectural drawing I did of that place, Dorje Khyung Dzong, which literally means the "vajra garuda fortress."[2]

The cave was very primitive, and apparently it was not a very good cave; it had a lot of leaks. It is said that due to the leaks, Trungpa's body was

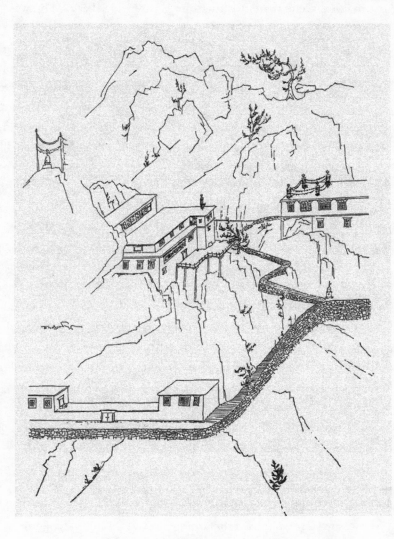

Dorje Khyung Dzong. Drawing by Chögyam Trungpa.

sometimes completely soaked in water up to his waist. According to the stories, he sat so still that birds made nests in his hair—which is not quite believable. However, it is said that birds began to nest in his hair because he never moved. He became part of the architectural design of that particular cave, like a tree. Being an important person, Trungpa had one attendant who was always there with him. Trungpa distrusted anybody who came to see him from the administration of Surmang, anybody representing the political scene there. Visiting him was terrible [because he was so nasty to visitors].

He practiced for six years. At the end of six years, he collapsed and lost consciousness. When he recovered from his collapse, he suddenly woke into a different frame of mind altogether. Some people thought he was completely crazy, at the level of schizophrenia, or whatever you might call it. Some people thought he had completely attained enlightenment. Seemingly, according to the favorable stories, he attained enlightenment. He behaved entirely differently. He was more fearless, powerful, enlightened—on that particular spot.[3]

His particular studies in the cave were involved with pushing beyond possessiveness of one's body, giving that particular concept up, giving it away. His practice was also involved with a sense of generosity. In this practice, your body is fed to the enemies or to the spirits, the ghosts, whatever you have. Whoever would like to take possession of your body, you give it to them completely. That particular technique is called *chö*, which literally means "cutting through." Cutting through involves giving up your security. After your security is given away, nothing replaces it. So there is a sense of complete leap, a sense of giving, constantly giving, opening: "If somebody would like to possess me or eat me up, go ahead. Kill me, eat me up! So what! You're welcome to do so." This technique actually originally developed out of the study of the *prajnaparamita*. The technique is based on no form, formlessness, no ego. Ego is empty, form is empty, and so forth.

The example set by Kunga Namgyal turned out to be one of the landmarks of the Trungpa lineage, which made the existence of the Trungpas more powerful. In addition to all the practice he did, he was also very scholarly, very learned. He composed something like twenty volumes of writings, which consisted of history, particularly the social science of the Tibetan tradition of that time, and commentaries on all kinds of books. He was also a great musician. He composed a lot of monastic musical tunes and developed various chants. Above all, he was a great contemplative person.

There was a change in the emphasis at this time. The tent culture began to become a more solid monastic situation, rather than being purely a caravan culture alone. More emphasis was put on the establishment of institutions, monasticism, and so forth.

Student: Rinpoche, I don't see the connection between prajnaparamita and chö.

Chögyam Trungpa Rinpoche: The connection is letting go. If there's no form, if there's no body, if everything's empty, so what? [That experience or understanding is the essence of both prajnaparamita and chö. —Ed.] It's letting go: "Take anything you want from me." That's basically the approach.

S: There still seems to be some sense of interaction [rather than just emptiness] there.

CTR: No. It's the prajnaparamita practice *in* practice, rather than in theory. "No nose, no eyes, no ears—take them all—literally take them."

S: Have a bite.

CTR: "Take it." Yes, that's the approach. So there's no point in holding back anyway, because they [the things you are giving up] are not really there.

S: Are the practices connected with chö quite specific? It sounds very general.

CTR: It's not very general. It's very specific. You go to a spot to be haunted; you let yourself be haunted on that particular spot. In that particular place that is supposedly a very haunting place, you are haunted. You give yourself completely up, over and over again. There were 108 places of that particular type that the Fourth Trungpa visited. If you feel that the place or the situation is eerie—or you can't handle the insects around you or the local people around you or anything else about the situation around you—you give it up, give it away. Would you like to do that?

S: So you specifically look for unpleasant situations?

CTR: Somewhat... Take a trip to Brooklyn! [*Laughter*]

S: Does that mean that when you take a trip to Brooklyn, you walk in the streets alone at night, in the middle of the night, and take your chances, even though it might be dangerous?

CTR: Something like that, something like that. But you have to be very composed. There is a lot of composure that takes place at the same time.

S: If you have your composure, then you'll be all right?

CTR: There's no promise. [*Laughter*]

S: It almost seems that Kunga Namgyal's life was a reaction to the solidification of the monastic situation. Is that a reasonable assumption?

CTR: Well, he wanted to be by himself. He wanted to be *himself*, that's all. I don't think he was particularly a beatnik or a hippie, trying to escape something, from that point of view. He was still interested and connected with what was happening at the monastery. He just needed to complete his meditation practice first. After he finished his training program, he presided over the monastic community, and at the same time he played a very important role in politics.

S: Regarding the practice of chö, it seems that in order to have composure in the situation, one would have already established an understanding of formlessness, of *shunyata*. Or should one try to reach an understanding of shunyata by trying to be composed in threatening situations, seeing how long one's composure will last?

CTR: You jump into situations first and then you relate with shunyata after that. However, without composure, it would be fatal.

S: So you open yourself to the haunting situations and the insects—

CTR: Or the Scotsmen.

S: The Scotsmen or the Irishmen or the Dutchmen—

CTR: Yup!

S: And then out of that situation of surrendering to that, would it lead to an understanding of shunyata?

CTR: Yes. Something like that.

S: Rinpoche, where does the sense of warmth and nonaggression come from in chö practice?

CTR: Both are simultaneously there within the experience of being haunted. There's no room for aggression if you're going to work with these situations all the time. Warmth is there because what you're doing, your practice, is based on benefiting all sentient beings. I'm sorry if that seems like a cliché. But actually it's true.

S: When Kunga Namgyal left the monastery, he was going out on his own to see how much he could take on by himself. Is that correct?
CTR: He was trying to see how much was *there*, rather than how much he could take.

S: You said that, in the time of Kunga Namgyal, there was an emphasis placed on the development of institutions and monasticism. How did their practice differ from the practice of their predecessors?
CTR: The predecessors' practice was still purely at an embryonic level. It was conquering Tibetan territory according to Buddhist principles. It was at a very early level or stage.

S: I don't understand how going to a haunted place and allowing yourself to be haunted, or for that matter meditating in a cave, benefits other sentient beings.
CTR: To begin with, there is no pollution created by your practice. If you work on yourself, it is much better than working with somebody else, haunting somebody else. You begin to develop a certain technique or realization within yourself, such that you don't actually pollute the rest of the psychological world that exists around you. When you attain some understanding, you don't pollute the rest of the world. If you use the rest of the world as the source of your development alone, people may give you good antidotes. At the same time, they are hurt by giving you antidotes. They are hurt as well, at the same time. So doing this by yourself is ecologically sound.

S: What was happening in Tibetan society that led to the monasteries taking a political role? It seems that some of the religious leaders weren't happy about that. Why did they do it?
CTR: I think the religious leaders were very happy about that, because they

could create a Buddhist nation, basically speaking. They could encourage everybody to sit, to practice, and to go along with the techniques that were already developed in society. The social norms of goodness could be continued and supported. They were quite happy, actually, and quite willing to do that. There was no problem particularly.

S: Would you describe the nature of the ongoing association between the Trungpa lineage and the Karmapas?

CTR: Each Trungpa lineage holder visited the Karmapa of that time. The gap was always bridged. There was no distance, no problem. The Karmapa always knew what was happening with the Trungpas, geographically, physically, and the Trungpas received encouragement and instructions from the Karmapas constantly. In fact, at times there was a lot of bonding, binding. The Karmapas bowed to or appreciated what was taking place in East Tibet with the powerful Kagyüpa administrators and powerful Kagyüpa teachers. Sometimes, due to Tibetan politics, very little was happening with the Kagyüpas in Central Tibet, where the Karmapas have their monastery. The Kagyü situation in Central Tibet was sometimes very scarce, very thin. A lot of the thickness, the solidity, of the Kagyü tradition took place in East Tibet. So the Karmapas were delighted that their colleagues in the East were working hard and that the dharma there was becoming more powerful.

CHAPTER SIX

Trungpas Five through Ten

Previously, we discussed the Fourth Trungpa, Kunga Namgyal, and how he was able to take time off from other responsibilities and practice a lot. He was not conducting too many seminars, not teaching courses at Naropa University, and not flying back and forth from various dharma centers. He had a chunk of time to practice, something like thirty years. Such fantastic luxury *he* had. [*Chuckles*]

Most of his time was spent trying to consolidate the teachings of the Kagyü lineage. Kunga Namgyal was one of the great editors of the Kagyü teachings, the Kagyü tradition. He wrote six hundred pages on the experience of mahamudra, as well as the training and discipline of how to get into mahamudra and how to understand mahamudra. Toward the end of his life, he also reorganized the administrative and political power of Surmang and the running of the organization. I would like to make it clear that the Fourth Trungpa wasn't particularly an anarchist who rebelled against authority or any kind of red tape. He had an enlightened approach to organization, which continued after he died.

After the death of the Fourth Trungpa, the situation was quite calm. His people in the administration began to fulfill various local functions. They were in charge of the district within Surmang province, as well as being responsible for maintaining the dharma practice of the Surmang tradition at the same time—which was quite a big task for them. However, they were able to do so.

The Fifth Trungpa was able to receive proper training. He was trained by a lot of the students of the previous Trungpa. All the necessary disciplines were already developed and available to him. The Fifth Trungpa's name was Tenpa Namgyal. He was born into a noble family in the local principality, and he was trained as a teacher. He became the ruler of that locality, as well as a powerful spiritual leader. He was known as an expert on the philosophy of Buddhism. He promoted the contemplative disciplines existing in the Surmang tradition. In those days, the Surmang monasteries were very much in the contemplative tradition. It was a contemplative community. There was very little need to set up any extra contemplative discipline. The monastic situation altogether was almost like a retreat center.

Tenpa Namgyal decided to make some changes, further transforming the traditional tent culture approach into a well-established, permanent setup. His court, as well as the fort of Adro Shelu-bum, were properly incorporated into a monastery. He received what is known as *hutoktu*,[1] an honorary degree or post as the teacher to the emperor of China. We still have the official seals that were presented to him. I was able to rescue them, to bring them with me from Tibet, and these seals are in Boulder at this point.[2] If you'd like to see them at a later time, you would be welcome to look at them. They're quite impressive seals that were presented by the Chinese emperor to the Fifth Trungpa as an imperial teacher.

At that point, the Fifth Trungpa's political power grew much larger. He was very well respected in that locality. He had a particular talent in dealing with the local kingdoms. Surmang belonged to the kingdom of Nangchen. The king of Nangchen was the ultimate power in that area. Surmang province was one of twenty-five provinces within that kingdom. The Fifth Trungpa, being an imperial teacher, had a great deal of power over that kingdom.

At that point, the Kagyü lineage in the country was going through a transformation. The Kagyüpas began to realize that in order to have higher spiritual participation in the country, they also had to have equally higher political participation. That particular process of combining the two was natural in Tibet. The Kagyüpas became politically active. It had nothing to do with the American notion of politics. In America when somebody runs for the presidency, somebody has to make up a story line and write speeches

Seals of the Trungpas.

for the candidate to deliver. You have to create a "Reelect the President" committee, or something of that nature. In this case, the Kagyüpa statesman had an inspired vision that was needed by the people of the particular locality. The leader was taking an active role in the spiritual welfare of the people, as well as taking care of their psychological and economic welfare. That is what was known as a politician in those days. In those days it wasn't so much that you had political parties running against each other or that you had the likelihood of running into problems like Watergate, for that matter.

Consequently, the Fifth Trungpa became a very affluent person and a very enlightened person at the same time. Because of his particular approach to dealing with the economy of the local villages and families all around the countryside, the Surmang province became an excessively wealthy province. The economy was built on timber and salt export. There were many talented businessmen and talented statesmen of all kinds. The Surmang province became a highly powerful province and a very wealthy province at that point.

The Central Tibetan government, which had nothing much to do with the province of Surmang, was quite shocked by the affluence. In Surmang the people were afraid of a possible political invasion by the Central Tibetan government. And in fact troops were sent out to invade and ransack Dütsi Tel and Namgyal Tse monasteries. They wanted to control the whole of Surmang province. The rest of the kingdom was left alone.

The Fifth Trungpa was imprisoned in the district capital of the Central Tibetan government.[3] The local capital representing the Central Tibetan government was called Chamdo. Tenpa Namgyal was put in prison with a number of others for five years, and his monasteries were ransacked. One of the excuses given by the Central Tibetan government for the invasion of one of the main Surmang monasteries was that it had a gold roof. They had created a gigantic shrine room, which was painted in gold leaf. A painting of the Buddha was drawn in vermillion paint over the gold. The Central Tibetan government said that this was illegal and that no monastery, no one in Tibet at all, was allowed to make such an ostentatious display of their wealth without receiving permission from the Central Tibetan government. This reasoning was quite absurd. Surmang was located in an entirely separate kingdom, politically and economically. Nevertheless, this took place.

When Tenpa Namgyal and his regent and many abbots and others were imprisoned, the kingdoms in that area didn't particularly lend him any support. The local government was afraid of possible warfare with Central Tibet. They didn't particularly help the Fifth Trungpa and his friends, his colleagues.

From the first year of the imprisonment of the Fifth Trungpa and his people, that province had constant droughts and constants mishaps with the harvest. At the end of the fourth year, everybody got very confused and concerned about a possible famine taking place. In the fifth year, famine actually took place in that area. People were starving. They didn't have grain to eat, and they had nowhere for the cows to graze. The whole country became completely dry. Supposedly this was the first time in history that this occurred in this area.

One of the cabinet ministers of the province said, "Maybe we should ask the Trungpa people to do something about this. Maybe we should ask them to create rain." Some people said, "Well, they're just a bunch of schmucks in prison, so what can we do?" On the other hand, somebody else said, "We've heard that they are very powerful people. Maybe it's because we imprisoned them that all these things and this chain reaction took place." All kinds of discussions took place.

Finally they decided to approach Trungpa himself and his colleagues.

However, the prisoners had achieved immense discipline in their practice at that point, and they didn't want to be disturbed at all. They were having a great time in prison. [*Laughter*] Trungpa had been able to finish three hundred million recitations of the Avalokiteshvara mantra. His friend, Chetsang Sung-rap Gyatso Rinpoche, who was also in prison, was painting thangkas.[4] He had completed something like one hundred beautiful thangka scrolls. We had them in our monastery, actually. They were beautifully painted. Another prisoner, Garwang Rinpoche, had written something like six volumes of commentary on mahamudra experience. So they were having a great time, and they didn't particularly want to be disturbed.

Then somehow this request from the government came: "You should make rain for us. Otherwise we're going to keep you in prison much longer, and you might be executed, killed." So Trungpa said, "Yes, sure. I could create rain for you." He asked to be taken to a local spring, a source of water, saying, "I could just go over there and do some little thing, if it helps. That will be fine." He washed his *mala* beads, his rosary. He dipped the beads in a fountain and washed them and sat there for a while. Then he went back to jail. Supposedly a lot of smoke arose; a sort of cloudy mist came out of the fountain and created clouds in the sky. There was fantastic rainfall.

That was in the late summer of that year. Everybody rejoiced and wanted to find out what had happened. The local people were very excited to finally have rainfall after five years. When they heard what had happened, that Trungpa did that, everybody unanimously demanded that Trungpa be freed from his imprisonment. Trungpa wasn't particularly happy about that. [*Laughter*] Prison was his retreat place. But he was given a pardon, and he was able to skip out of his retreat, so to speak. [*Chuckles*] He was given back all his privileges and his monastery.

Such political situations took place frequently. In that era, the Gelukpa kingdom of the Central Tibetan government was paranoid and constantly tried to control any area where a local teacher had power over people. The Central Tibetan government regarded that as very bad. At some point, a regent of the Karmapa lineage, who was called Shamar, was beheaded. Supposedly his head was buried underneath the shrine at Lhasa so that everybody would walk over it while they were on pilgrimage. All kinds of things like that took place. It's true that this went on, and it's terrible that these kinds of things would take place in a supposedly Buddhist world. Nevertheless, those problems existed.

The Fifth Trungpa was victorious. He was still respected by the Chinese emperor as an imperial teacher. There were no other particular highlights of the story of the Fifth Trungpa, and he passed away peacefully.

Then we have the Sixth Trungpa, about whom very little is known. He died when he was very young. Some time after he was discovered as the Trungpa tulku, when he was about eighteen or nineteen years old, one of his students was carrying him to help him cross a bridge. They both slipped and fell, and he died on the spot. So much for the Sixth Trungpa.

The Seventh Trungpa was a very intelligent person who studied a great deal. But he also died young, around the age of twenty-five. There's no particular monument that he left behind, except that he wrote lots of poetry. Many of his poems were lost, but some of them were kept in the archives of the Surmang monasteries. It was a very romantic type of poetry, somewhat adolescent but insightful nevertheless. It was not particularly good as poetry. He was developing, but he died very young.

The Eighth Trungpa's name was Gyurme Tenphel. He was a very eccentric person and a great artist. He was supposed to have had a mustache and a beard, which is unusual for Tibetans. He was a very articulate person in terms of visual dharma, so to speak. He was a great calligrapher and a great painter. At the same time, he was a great composer. He produced music for monastic chants. He also edited and collected the works of the previous Trungpas and of the Surmang tradition in general. He collected the songs and life stories of Trung Ma-se as well. He also paid a visit to the Fourteenth Karmapa.

The Eighth Trungpa was one of the chief instructors, teachers, and possessors of *The Tibetan Book of the Dead*. When *The Tibetan Book of the Dead* was first discovered by Karma Lingpa, he presented it to the Eighth Trungpa and asked him to take care of this book and said that Gyurme Tenphel should actually help in promoting this particular teaching. So the Eighth Trungpa became very powerful in presenting the whole source of *The Tibetan Book of the Dead*. We, as Surmang people, actually regard *The Tibetan Book of the Dead* as belonging to us as one of the Surmang traditions. If you read in the book when it recounts the lineage of *The Tibetan*

Book of the Dead, it mentions that it belongs to the Surmang tradition of contemplative discipline within the Kagyü discipline.[5]

I've seen some of the illuminated manuscripts and artwork by Gyurme Tenphel. They were fantastic and very beautiful. His handwriting was impeccable. He seemed to have artistic tendencies. He was also a very gentle person. Supposedly he had two fights during his whole life. Once a cat jumped on his dish of food. He pushed the cat aside and he got very angry. The cat was trying to lick his soup or something. [*Chuckling*] The second time, his attendant cut his bamboo pen, his calligraphy pen, in the wrong way. Trungpa lost his temper. He lost his temper twice in his life. Isn't that shocking? [*Laughter*]

He was very gentle and artistic, a well-meaning person. We had some of his art in our monastery. His taste was extraordinarily rich, in terms of creating mountings for thangkas. He would buy brocades and use them to mount the scrolls, and he would cover books with silk scarves of all kinds. His taste was impeccable and very rich, wealthy, and with a somewhat aristocratic flavor. He was supposed to have come from a wealthy aristocratic family.

Then we have the Ninth Trungpa, who was very special. All the Surmang people loved him a lot, but he didn't do anything at all in his life. [*Laughter*] He was educated in the traditional style, nevertheless. He spent his whole life drinking Tibetan tea and taking snuff, sunning himself in the courtyards and chatting with his old friends. The only literary work he composed in all his life was a four-line poem supplicating Mahakala. It was very simple, actually. It goes like this:

Chief protector of the teachings
I supplicate you, Mahakala, the four-armed one.
Accept this offering.
Fulfill the four karmas.

That's it! [*Laughter*]

He was the least charismatic person among all the Trungpas, throughout the whole lineage. He was just sort of a basic good old Surmang redneck. [*Laughter*] Nothing very much happened with him at all. He enjoyed

having a sit-together situation in certain spots in the courtyard where usually, particularly on winter days, the sun would shine. He used to have
those sit-together sessions with people, in whatever particular spot was
best, where they would drink tea and have snuff and gossip about little
things. That's our Ninth Trungpa.

The Tenth Trungpa, my own predecessor, was quite a different person.
Not deliberately but coincidentally, he was born to a local chieftain of Surmang. He was raised with very strict discipline by his uncles, as well as his
tutors, his bursars, secretaries, and whatever you have. In the early part of
his life, he took everything extraordinarily seriously. He took everything
in the Kagyü lineage very seriously—his *ngöndro* practice, his *shamatha-
vipashyana* practice, and everything. He did every practice one by one very
successfully.

He didn't like being told what to do. Particularly, he felt that people were
trying to make him into a good money-making person. Traditionally, the
monastery set up a winter trip, a summer trip, and an autumn trip to collect donations from the locality. That had recently become traditional. During the summer trip, the monks would collect dry cheese and butter. In the
autumn, they would collect certain sorts of turnips and potatoes, vegetables
of that nature. And during the winter trip, the monks would collect grains
of all kinds, predominantly wheat and barley, with some beans and peas, or
whatever was available. So the poor Tenth Trungpa was pushed to make
these trips all the time. It was always time to make the next round of trips.
That became problematic for the Tenth Trungpa, and he didn't like it. He
didn't want to constantly involve himself with the work of collecting donations while not practicing anymore.

One night, he decided to leave. This is all written about in *Born in Tibet*.
You can read the story of the Tenth Trungpa there, which is quite colorful
in some sense. At this time, he decided to leave his monastery and his camp
and try to seek teachings from Jamgön Kongtrül the Great. He managed
to do so, and having received some teachings from Jamgön Kongtrül, he
decided to stay with him for a long period of time, continuing his practice,
his discipline, and his study.

He was very hard up at that time. The monastery wanted to lure him
back, so they didn't give him any resources. There was not even enough

butter for him to create a butter lamp so that he could read the scriptures in the evening. He had to buy sticks of incense and try to read the texts, studying and memorizing them by the glow of an incense stick. Supposedly, when the Tenth Trungpa was memorizing texts and trying to practice, he tied his hair to the ceiling with a cord, and he stuck nettles around himself on his bed. If he dozed and started to fall over, he would be pulled up by his hair or he'd be stung by the nettles. He kept himself alive by practicing constantly under the great Jamgön Kongtrül. It was a very rare situation to become a student of Jamgön Kongtrül. The Tenth Trungpa became one of the world-renowned teachers of the Kagyü tradition.

He also had his political problems. The same old problem kept coming back again and again in our province. Our monastery kept being attacked by a local Geluk monastery. They raised legal points questioning Surmang's power over them. The Tenth Trungpa spent something like three months in the local capital, Jyekundo,[6] arguing his case. There were no lawyers like we have these days. The Tenth Trungpa had to create his whole case by writing out each point one by one. There was nobody else actually able to compose this literature for him, so he had to write everything out at night and present the points during the day. He spent three months presenting the case for the survival of Surmang Monastery, fighting for its existence.

He asked his friends for suggestions and help. He asked those who were also well versed in Tibetan law to contribute. A famous line came out of this from one of the local chieftains, who told him, "It is OK even for a lama or a tulku or a rinpoche to argue a court case. That's fine. But you must accept one thing, which is that you should tell the body of truth with the tentacles of a lie. Otherwise, if you are constantly truthful and honest, you won't win your court case." [*Chuckles*] This was actually very helpful to the Tenth Trungpa in winning his court case.

When he won the case, this infuriated a lot of people in the locality, particularly the Gelukpa factions in the province. His monastery was attacked by the troops of the Central Tibetan government. The monastery was completely burned down and looted, and the Tenth Trungpa was taken prisoner. He was eventually rescued by friends. The general of the Central Tibetan government, who was also a local king, the king of Lhathok, saved him.[7] It's an interesting situation that the political neuroses of the country were still taking place even in those days, which was in the 1920s. Even that late in time, there were still these political problems taking place.

Having recovered control of his monastery, the Tenth Trungpa rebuilt it completely, fully, much better than it had been before. It had been burned down and looted, and the libraries were destroyed. Some people said that it was great that the monastery was destroyed, because then they could create a fresh situation, much grander. That actually was the case at Surmang. In rebuilding the monastery, the ambition of the Tenth Trungpa was to change the shape of the situation altogether. Instead of having a monastery alone, he also established a contemplative community center to go along with the monastic center, with possibilities for a study situation to take place within that. Through this process, the Tenth Trungpa reestablished monasticism and contemplative discipline at the same time.

The Tenth Trungpa died at the age of sixty-three, still trying to raise funds for the monastic establishment. [*Chuckles*] The monastery was doing OK, but it still needed a financial boost to provide more oomph. He was an example of a hard worker, a political visionary, and a powerful person who was able to win others over. He could conquer someone else's false concepts. He was a great, dedicated person in the contemplative tradition, who united all this in one situation. He was such a powerful, open, and fearless person. One chaos after another chaos occurred in his life, yet he was still able to hold on to his basic integrity. I've been told that he had fantastic integrity. So there we are [*chuckles*]—those are the Trungpas.

Student: Can you say something about the different incarnations and how they found the different Trungpas?

Chögyam Trungpa Rinpoche: It was the same process as with myself, in some sense. There's often a message left behind by the previous incarnation, saying where that person is going to be reborn. You follow that instruction, basically. Sometimes, if no message had been left, you would ask the head of the order, which was usually the Karmapa, and he would give you directions. In my case, the Tenth Trungpa didn't leave any directions, but the Sixteenth Karmapa gave some indications. He said that the particular place where the Eleventh Trungpa would be born was a house that faces the south. The family would have a brown dog, and they would have a daughter, as well as a young son in the family. This son would be the Eleventh Trungpa. The Karmapa gave the names of the father and mother. The monks found that everything fitted that particular description. So by following that tradition, everything continued that way. It's not so much a continuing soul or ego, but it's some kind of deposit of intelligence, a possible way of reawakening the intelligence, which takes place.

S: I have two questions. One refers to this "mishap" you spoke of again today. I'm wondering, does a mishap always have to be a kind of negative experience, a painful experience, or can it also be a positive or good experience in some sense?

CTR: Well, usually we don't use the word *mishap* to refer to a good experience.

S: Does it always have to be something you're not too happy about—

CTR: It's somewhat unpleasant.

S: I'm also wondering about the energy that keeps various lines or tulkus going, particularly as regards someone like the Ninth Trungpa. You said he didn't seem to do much. Also, the Sixth and the Seventh Trungpas died very early. What is it about them that kept the lineage going? Why didn't it stop then?

CTR: I think it's some fundamental integrity that is always there.

S: And that was initiated after the First Trungpa?

CTR: Yes.

S: In the last lecture, you were talking about students at the time of the Fourth Trungpa, saying that they sat a lot more than we do now. I was wondering if you could say something about the approach to sitting and discipline that's different now from in the past?

CTR: According to the tradition that directs us, it says that people of future generations in the dark age should sit more than they did in the golden days, the golden age.

S: Was it so golden?

CTR: Yes, in terms of there being fewer temptations. The world was not particularly geared or oriented for pleasure. The world was a manual world, rather than a mechanical world.

S: It also seems that at this time you're not particularly encouraging students to sit much more than what we're already doing. Is that just because we're not ready for it?

CTR: I think I'll be doing much more—or you will be. [*Laughter*]

S: I've been thinking throughout this seminar about all the people around the Trungpas. There are no particular stories about them, and somehow they didn't make it to the big time, you know. [*Laughter*]

CTR: Which people are you talking about?

S: Well, the ten or twenty or hundred or two hundred students who were around the Trungpas. Thinking along this same line, what is it that makes an enlightened person an enlightened person? We have these stories about the Trungpas, who in some sense are very heroic and did heroic deeds. At the same time, I know that for myself, I'm not particularly putting nettles around myself if I'm falling asleep. In fact, quite the opposite.

CTR: Quite the opposite? [*Laughter*]

S: Is there some suggestion being made that some sort of heroism is absolutely necessary?

CTR: It's not trying to make yourself loud and polluting things around you. But as a practitioner, some kind of heroism is necessary. That is to say, it's not trying to proclaim yourself as better than somebody else. At the same time, it seems to be good to have some kind of heroism within yourself. It's not so much based on the example of each president in this country, who says, "I'm making history, and this is fantastic. I won the elections," or whatever. But some kind of heroism is needed, that you are doing what you are doing. It seems to be very simple. It's heroism toward yourself, rather than anything else.

S: I'd like to ask a further question about the relationship between the work that the Trungpas had to do and their practice. You've talked about the relationship between their lives as administrators and their lives as practitioners, which seemed generally to be very simpleminded. They went through a period of intense practice, and then having developed somewhat, they could afford to get into running Surmang. Many of your students, on the other hand, seem to constantly be adapting our practice schedule, attempting to sensibly adapt it, to some kind of ongoing work. Then we experience emergencies. There always seem to be developments we're going through that suddenly make it incredibly difficult to do intensive practice. Then the question arises: Is it just my lack of organization, or is this a special situation where I have to practice less because there's so much work to do? Should I feel guilty? You expect that kind of question to come up only when you're given a sudden unexpected and heavy amount of responsibility. But that kind of responsibility seems to occur twice a year, year after year. What kind of attitude should we have toward that? [The student is referring to the exigencies of running a practice center.—Ed.]

CTR: Interestingly, at this point administration and work rely on mechanical devices, literally mechanical devices, and efficient phone conversations. If you want to talk to somebody across the country, you don't have to go there, or you don't have to send a messenger there and pay for his food and organize his life situation. If you want to heat the room, you don't have to employ a group of people to make a fire for you. No one has to constantly use a bellows to keep a fire going to keep us warm. No one has to hold up torches instead of using lightbulbs. From that point of view, a lot of things have been solved. Because a lot is taken care of, therefore a lot of practice and further intelligence play a very important part. The administrative situation at this point is just purely pushing a button, compared with the middle ages of the Tibetan world. It's a very, very light responsibility. You don't have to administrate a lot of people. You just do things based on your own level of intelligence. From that point of view, it seems to be very simple.

At this point, the administration and the practice come together, quite rightly so, because there are not so many management problems as there were at the time of the Tenth Trungpa or the previous Trungpas. Instead of involving something like three hundred people working together to build a house, now we have a very few people doing the work together, because a lot of things are controlled by mechanisms, machinery, electricity, and everything.

S: Well, for the few people who are doing these things, perhaps because of the industrial aids, which make it more efficient than before, they might go through a period of time when they can meditate four and a half hours a day or take a retreat. If you're living in the city, you build up the money and then you can do an intensive practice period. But suddenly a period of time will come when practice is cut way down or cut out entirely, except with some extraspecial effort.

CTR: Extraspecial effort is always important. [*Laughter*] Otherwise nothing would happen, you know. You can't just slide into the airplane, like your baggage that is checked at the airport and loaded automatically onto the plane. It's not automatic that now you have time to sit, now you have time to work—things don't happen that way, anyway. There's always room for you to play the role manually, and understand the whole thing in a manual way, which is always going to be harsh truth, sooner or later, later or sooner.

S: Harsh truth?

CTR: Harsh truth.

S: I don't understand the last part of what you were saying about the manual way.

CTR: You can't just go along with automation. You always have problems of fitting yourself into the right socket. It's always manual—finding the right socket.

CHAPTER SEVEN

The Eleventh Trungpa

T HE TRADITION of the Trungpas evolved to its best capability in presenting what is known as the "three disciplines." These are the disciplines of exertion, meditation, and knowledge or prajna, presented at their best. The Trungpa lineage became one of the most genuine lineages in the Buddhist world of Tibet. There were all kinds of sociological problems—social upheavals, political intrigues, and economic problems within the community—that interfered with the execution of teaching the dharma. Nevertheless, the lineage of the Trungpas turned out to be one of the highlights of East Tibet, and it was also a central point or focus for Tibet as a whole.

The Central Tibetan government, which was very interested in political power, had to bend down to the efforts of the Trungpas. At the beginning of the twentieth century, the practice of the Central Tibetan government was to try to centralize power in order to keep political control over the rest of Tibet. The Surmang traditions became painfully prickly and threatening. I could give you an American analogy, I suppose. If the White House didn't have a sauna bath, any wealthy households or householders would not be allowed to have one. That was the kind of political poverty that had developed. This mentality was partly governed by mistrust and paranoia toward the Kagyü tradition, which was regarded by some as the order of crazy people. If anybody from this crazy Kagyü world began to do something funny or strange, the Central Tibetan government couldn't cope with it and felt they should clamp down. Basically speaking, they were afraid of crazy wisdom. Crazy wisdom is one of the most promising things for us in the Kagyü lineage, and it was very prominent in the general psychology of Surmang.

As far as the government of Central Tibet was concerned, this part of East Tibet was governed by a bunch of whatnots. At the same time, as far as those in the Kagyü tradition were concerned, there was no particular antagonism or resentment per se. The Kagyü approach was somewhat like the hippies' mentality toward the police force, or the approach of freestyle people—freaks versus the rednecks. It is an interesting social study. Even these days in exile, there is some measure of caution. Only certain Tibetans from the refugee camps are allowed to leave India, namely those who don't belong to the crazy wisdom lineage. [*Chuckles*]

That's a very interesting point. The Eleventh Trungpa was able to sneak out of a tightly controlled political situation in India. There was no bribery involved and no need to prove myself, but it just simply occurred because of the plain old facts. When I received a grant from the Spalding Trust to attend Oxford University, I applied to the Tibetan Government in Exile to study in England, saying, "I have this grant, and I would like to leave India and go to England." It was very simple and direct. Until then, I had been employed as a spiritual adviser in a school for young tulkus in India, and I was seen as a would-be candidate for good things. [*Laughter*] I had tried to lead three hundred refugees out of Tibet, unsuccessfully for the majority of them, but still nevertheless, I made an attempt to help many people get out of the country, and some of us succeeded. There was a promising future for this young man, who was able to relate with foreign languages. I was a bright young guy who had studied a lot and seemed to comprehend everything about the West. So there was no reason to prevent this bright young man from leaving the country. They allowed me to go out—which was not a particularly big deal. It was a natural decision. I was fantastically yielding and seemingly very nationalistic, and all the rest of it. So there was no reason to prevent me from leaving the country.

It might be an interesting sidetrack to discuss how Tibetan politics work in the present day [1975]. The living situation for many Tibetans is quite wretched these days. Those who are still under the protection of the

Tibetan Government in Exile benefit from this a great deal. A few little internal political sparks or fireworks still go on. This is not so bad, actually. It's what is needed. Otherwise the whole situation would completely flop, like a dead horse. People do their best to energize themselves by their involvement with politics. It's a way for them to survive, I suppose.

I don't want to talk too much about the Eleventh Trungpa, because that is myself. But since I have personal experience of my life, this will be a firsthand account. If you don't mind, it would be interesting to discuss some little highlights, although it might be beating one's own drum or something like that.

The training and discovery of the Eleventh Trungpa took place beginning around the fortieth year of the twentieth century.[1] The death of the Tenth Trungpa shook a lot of people, including the Sixteenth Karmapa and important members of the Kagyü tradition. The Central Tibetan government had fairly recently just about finished destroying the Surmang monasteries. So when the death of the Tenth Trungpa occurred, it was not particularly pleasant for them either. They had their particular guilt about things that had occurred.

The Tenth Trungpa left no directions for how to rediscover the Eleventh. So the monastic committee of Surmang had to go to visit His Holiness the Karmapa in Central Tibet. According to his vision—which we already discussed briefly in the last talk—this particular child had been born in a house, or actually an encampment, five days' journey from the Surmang Monastery. The place was named so-and-so; the province was named so-and-so; the family had a brown dog; the father's name was Yeshe Dargye; the mother's name was Chung Tzo; there were two children, a sister and a younger brother. The younger brother would be the Eleventh Trungpa.[2]

The monks from Surmang searched and searched. They selected all kinds of names of different villagers, which they brought back to the Karmapa, but none of them was right. Finally on their third search, they found the place and discovered my parents' names. They took this information back and presented it to the Karmapa, and with one short glance His Holiness the Sixteenth Karmapa said, "This is the right person; you've found him." [*Laughs; laughter*]

The monks took a selection of articles that had belonged to the last Trungpa with them on their search, as well as objects and household articles that belonged to others. And when these things were presented to the Eleventh Trungpa, he passed all the tests completely by selecting the objects that had belonged to his predecessor. They also showed him a list of the six realms and told him to point to the realm he came from: "If you come from the hell realm, point to that. If you come from the hungry ghost realm, point to that. If you come from the human realm, point to that. If you come from the *asura* realm, the realm of the jealous gods, point to that." And so on. The Eleventh Trungpa pointed to the human realm, of course. Having passed all of these tests, so to speak, this little boy turned out to be the fateful Eleventh Trungpa.

I was brought back to the monastery with my parents when I was about eighteen months old. His Holiness Karmapa was visiting in the locality at this time. He was there to study with his tutors and teachers in East Tibet. So the enthronement ceremony for the Eleventh Trungpa was conducted by His Holiness himself. He also conducted the first cutting of the hair, which is a sign of becoming a monk and a Buddhist. It's kind of a baptism ceremony.

My education began very simply, around the age of five. I think I may have been four and a half, something like that, when I started learning to read and write. My tutor had a scar on his forehead. He was a bald-headed guy who was invited from the province next to Surmang to come and train me. He had been a disciple of the previous Trungpa. I remember one winter morning the snow was very thick outside, and people were trying to push it off the flat roof of the monastery. I was woken up earlier than usual and I had an early breakfast. "This is a very special occasion," somebody said, and they lit incense and prostrated to the shrine. I was brought into the shrine room and other people said their little "Hey nonni-nonni"— their religious things—in the shrine room. Then I was brought back into the living room and told, "Now you are going to learn to read." First I learned to read "ka, kha, ga, nga, ca, cha, ja, nya" and all the other letters of the Tibetan alphabet. I was told that "ka" looks like somebody walking on three legs ཀ, and "kha" is somebody with a big mouth and their tongue hanging out ཁ. "Ga" is like an animal walking ག, and "nga" looks like a worm ᠵ. They gave me all these little descriptions of the letters, and it was very enjoyable at the time.

As a child, you wonder what's going to happen when you begin to learn. Are they going to switch your mind around or inside out and show you something different inside? Apparently they are just going to show you these designs. It was OK. And it was quite light and relaxed that morning. I was waiting for when the actual beating was going to take place. [*Laughter*] It didn't happen for several days, but then, slowly but surely, it came along. [Corporal punishment was an expected part of the educational process.—Ed.]

Learning was quite simple. I was moved into the retreat center, Dorje Khyung Dzong, which was created by the Tenth Trungpa. It was very bleak up in the retreat. Winter was continuing, and snow was falling constantly, again and again. Dogs were barking in the distance. You could hear the retreatants ringing their gongs and gathering their drums in the evenings for the Mahakala *pujas*. Apart from that, nothing was very exciting or entertaining. At the same time, the learning process was quite exciting. You were constantly challenged by little things. However, your mind would tend to wander a great deal to something else. A child's mind is constantly drifting to something else.

For instance, I used to get very fascinated by the grain of the paper on which the alphabet was written. The letters were written on handmade paper with lots of grain in it that made designs. Sometimes I would confuse the designs on the paper with the alphabet. Sometimes I would make out a little tiger or a little dragon or snake in the designs, all kinds of little things like that. But still, my education went on OK.

Suddenly, everybody was very excited about me. I didn't quite know what it was all about. My tutor said, "You learned the whole alphabet right away. Now we can teach you the next thing." We went on to training in spelling and reading, which went on for a long time.

This particular tutor was a very kind person. He used to tell me stories about Milarepa, Padmasambhava, the previous Trungpas, and lots of other lineage figures. It was very exciting. I used to like to ask him questions, partly because I was trying to avoid studying too much, and partly I was interested in hearing stories about all these people. It was very interesting.

On several occasions, lots of occasions, my tutor lost his temper. More likely in his case he actually thought that he *should* lose his temper. When he would lose his temper, he would take his time before he actually beat me. He used to get up and light a stick of incense first. Then he would go out and wash his hands. Then he prostrated three times, and then he would begin to beat me. That ceremony was a very intense one. After a while, he didn't have to even go as far as washing his hands. He would just light the incense, and I would know the whole thing that was coming. [*Laughter*]

At a certain point, when I was about nine, the monastic committee and particularly the bursar, or the secretary, thought that my tutor was being too kind, telling me too many stories and not teaching enough. The committee decided to appoint someone else to replace him, which as far as I was concerned was a terrible idea, [*chuckles*] and I still think so! [*Laughter*]

The new tutor was a man with a reputation for immense accomplishment in training young kids. His own nephew and his relatives and all of his students became great learned people. But at the same time he was very hot tempered, short-tempered, and he was very strict and wouldn't allow me any space to have a good time. I rarely heard stories about anything from him. He was my tutor for quite a long time.

At a certain point, I began to surpass his talent. My handwriting was better than his, and my reading ability was better than his. He still worked to create a better version of me. His help was very powerful. We had at least three scenes every day, where I was either being hit or being pinched or having things thrown at me. That was constantly taking place. In between times, he was very loving, nice, and kind, very fatherly. He would speak in a high-pitched voice, praising me. "Oooooo, nice Rinpoche, oooooo," or what have you. [*Laughs; laughter*]

We had quite a lot of fun toward the end of my development. He was very proud and kept on gossiping with others, telling them stories about how well I was doing with him. But whenever I was in front of him, he would say, "Still not so good. That's terrible." That was an interesting experience.

At a certain point, people in the monastic community as well as my attendants—which consisted of a food server, a person in charge of interviews, a person who screened the people who came out and in, and a person who was in charge of my general welfare—all of these people began to get very tired of my tutor because of his short-temperedness and how he constantly created scenes. A very hot situation took place.

One evening as I lay down to go to sleep, my tutor said, "I have to talk to you, I'm thinking of resigning." This was when I was about thirteen. "You seem to have learned what I have to teach you, and I have no more to teach you. But if you are interested, I could stay on, if you like." [*Chuckles*] My response was, "That's good." And I told him, "You did a great job, and I appreciate it, but I think you should go." [*Laughter*] He swallowed, and you could hear him swallowing his own inbreath. The next day he presented his resignation to the committee, and the day after that he packed, and the day after that he left. This gave me a very interesting feeling. I felt somewhat terrible, and at the same time I experienced fantastic freedom. Now I could do what I wanted. But I couldn't think of what I wanted to do, particularly. Just the same old thing. [*Laughter*] However, it was a fantastic experience of rediscovering freedom. I'm sure this is similar to American kids finally leaving home or running away, or something like that.

The situation of my work, practice, and study continued after that. At that point, the situation became very natural to me. Particularly, my own little hesitations, problems of laziness, feelings of inadequacy—all those feelings of being a dumb person were completely uplifted. There was a sense of realizing that whatever further things I wanted to do, I could do them. A sense of delight and sort of dancing in the learning situation took place. This situation continued, particularly when I studied with my root teacher Jamgön Kongtrül at his monastery, Sechen (known as Jamgön Kongtrül of Sechen). There was a *khenpo*, Khenpo Gangshar, at Jamgön Kongtrül's monastery who was one of the teachers, or professors, and you had your own tutors for studying. The learning situation at Sechen Monastery was very energetic. I felt inadequate at the beginning. But I learned that as soon as you are able to click in to one particular point, you begin to cultivate that, and from that you begin to build everything around it. You begin to realize that you have a lot of responsibilities and a lot of capabilities taking place simultaneously, which is fantastic.

Meeting Jamgön Kongtrül was remarkable, and I think it's worth telling this particular story. Throughout the whole time I was with my tutor and with other people at Surmang, they were telling me stories about their

Chögyam Trungpa (right) with the Khenpo from Sechen, Khenpo Gangshar,
who was an important guru for Trungpa Rinpoche.

admiration for people who had died, great teachers they had met who lived
in the past. I had never met any of them. According to these stories, the
whole spiritual thing is that you have to be a completely religious person.
Even if you are not, you should pretend. You pretend to be good, and you
keep smiling at everybody. You say nice things to everybody, and you half
close your eyes all the time, as if you are pretending to meditate all the
time. That was the kind of story I heard. But then, meeting Jamgön Kongtrül, I began to actually see what people really meant. It was not so much
that he half closed his eyes all the time or behaved in a saintly way particularly. He joked around, he was very jolly, and he was very kind and soft and
insightful. Sometimes he didn't even sit upright. I had been told to always
sit upright. He lay down in his seat and he accommodated people. There
was immense power coming to you from that presence.

Jamgön Kongtrul, Chögyam Trungpa's root guru.
Photo by Chögyam Trungpa.

From that time onward, I would say that the journey was very definite and really committed. Before that particular point, I felt that I was being made to be a charlatan and asked to make a fool of myself. This happened particularly when I was told to say certain things to visiting dignitaries. I would be virtually made to memorize the whole conversation. The monks would say, "Then he will say that, you will say that, and then he will say that, and you will say that." Well, the problem was that the other people wouldn't say the things that you expected them to say. [*Laughter*] So then I was completely lost, and there were occasional confusions like that involved. [*Laughter*] At first I thought that even those people were programmed as well, so everything should be synchronized. But somehow that wasn't the case, as I realized. I felt envious of them that they could speak freely, while I had to memorize what to say. So it was very interesting meeting Jamgön Kongtrül, who was the real embodiment of sanity.

I think the early part of my upbringing is the important point. There is not really much point in going on. We could go on for twenty-four hours, but there's no particular point in going through the rest of it. The interesting point here is how you begin on an ordinary level, on this sort of imbecile-child level, and from that how you begin to click into the various stages of sophistication, sanity, and a visionary kind of world. That theme seems to play a very important part in my life. How can you emulate a greater person? By imitating them? By memorizing their speech? By pretending? None of those seems to work. One just has to *be* it, on a very simple level.

The dreams of all of the Trungpas were to propagate Buddhism, just as the dreams of all of those in the Kagyü tradition were to conquer foreign territories in the name of the Practicing Lineage, in the name and in the style of basic sanity. The general idea is that the presentation of Buddhism should be carried forward somewhat in the manner of crazy wisdom. So here we are! Buddhism is in America at this point.

Student: Several nights ago you talked about the deliberate practice of exposing oneself to being haunted. You mentioned that this kind of practice requires a great deal of composure. I take it that this composure is not the usual sense of composure, which is some sort of cool head that comes from the confidence that you are going to be OK. What is the composure that you were talking about based on? What does it rely on?

Chögyam Trungpa Rinpoche: Very interestingly, this kind of composure is based on bluntness, which is not the usual idea of composure. It's not supposed to be blunt usually, but it's supposed to be very delicate. This sense of composure is bluntness, not in the sense of vomiting out everything, but bluntness in the sense of fearlessness. You are not allowing any kind of bullshit to get in between the two situations, but just simply presenting the facts as they are.

S: One other question: The word *haunting* brought to mind the experiences we have when we sit a lot. When we sit longer and longer, our trips become pretty apparent. Some sort of superwatcher seems to go on, and one tends to feel somewhat desolate and haunted by that. Is this kind of technique recommended in a situation such as you described? Should we be that deliberate?

CTR: Yes. Deliberate.

S: Deliberately abandoning, giving in to that sort of haunted situation?

CTR: Wouldn't hurt a flea.

S: I would like to ask you some questions about the two methods that you mentioned: working with mishaps, and the cutting through that you just described now. I gather that, being in the Kagyü lineage, we inherit mishaps. The point is not to try to get to a state where there are no mishaps around you, but maybe to try to get to the state where you can use mishaps almost as a means of locomotion. You might use them to move forward. Like explosions in an engine, the mishaps would drive you forward. Would it be something like that?

CTR: I think so, but not to the extent of self-destructiveness.

S: No, but like energy.

CTR: Yes, definitely. In other words, the Kagyü lineage is not afraid of any mishaps. They welcome them.

S: They get more mileage per mishap than any other lineage on the path. [*Laughs; laughter*]

CTR: Absolutely. Otherwise, the Kagyüpas wouldn't be taking journeys out to foreign territories to convert people into Buddhism.

S: Then I also wanted to ask you about the cutting through. It seems it might almost be an extension of the mishap principle of movement, only taking it a whole step further. A mishap is something you wait for, until it happens to you, and then you work with it. With the cutting through it's almost as if you would anticipate and walk into a—

CTR: Sometimes cutting through becomes the vanguard of mishaps, but still that cutting through is the right thing to do. Yes.

S: When you described the composure as bluntness, it reminded me of something you talked about at your "Tibetan Buddhist Path" course at Naropa in 1974. You talked about magic, and one aspect of it being the ability to go through obstacles by means of crushing them with a certain bluntness, like the bluntness of a hand-hewn rock knife. This sounds like the same thing.

CTR: I think so. Yes. You have a good memory. That's pretty good, sir.[3]

S: I remembered it because of the strong image. It makes sense to me.

[*Laughter*] I would like to know what the connection is between practicing
meditation and this sense of using mishaps and cutting through, and between
those two things and the state known as the "state of nonmeditation."

CTR: I don't want to go too far with that discussion here.

S: I'm sorry, what do you mean?

CTR: I wouldn't go too far with discussing that state of nonmeditation.

S: Well, it seems that with the cutting through, there's a question of leaping
into something. Would you rather not talk about that state?

CTR: That's not particularly for discussing in public, shall we say. That discussion comes later, as you progress further on the path. [*Laughs*]

S: Finally, would you say that the mishap situation is working with hope
and that the cutting-through situation is working with fear?

CTR: Yes, that's right. That's good actually.

S: Each of the Trungpas seems to have a distinct style. I believe you mentioned how some students begin to develop a certain style in relating to
the teachings. I was wondering if there is a style of relating to the teacher
and the teachings that is somehow different from the way we approach
other things in life? Is there something specifically happening in the
student-teacher situation that affects our style of relating to the whole
process?

CTR: I think the style is largely based on national behavior, or just the
general karma that we are stuck with, that we're in. How we relate depends
on the larger situation, the general karma that we've created. It's like how
to relate with the winterness in Vermont or the Karmê Chöling-ness of
the situation. [The seminar took place at the Karmê Chöling practice center in Vermont.—Ed.] You know, you can't just change the whole situation completely at all. We have to adapt to that situation. In the summer,
when we have a water shortage, we might have to bathe in the lake, and
flush the toilets less because of a shortage of water, or whatever. Those situations are timely. The style is not particularly an individual version, but it's
related with how the situation is handled, how the situation has evolved
around you.

S: What exactly do you mean by how you relate to the situation around you
in terms of style?

CTR: Well, you are *there*, in the situation. So you can't be here [somewhere else], because of the crowd, or the distance, between there and here.

S: I wanted to get into the question of having a certain style of relating to a situation. I'm basically asking about the Trungpas. What makes a Trungpa?

CTR: What makes Trungpa is what makes Surmang. Surmang is Trungpa. Trungpa is Surmang, in some sense. You know, that situation or that kind of connection is developing here, too. Generally, the style of the teachings is based on the national psychology and national attitude. Either that psychology makes things completely workable for the development of the lineage, or if you have the completely wrong handle, or the wrong end of the stick [i.e., if the national psychology and the teachings are at odds], things are constantly destructive, and obstacles of all kinds occur to you.

S: I've heard a rumor that you are supposed to be the last of the Trungpas. Is this because you have an idea about what's going to happen in America? Is it that the style of the Trungpas is just not workable in America, and a new style has to be developed?

CTR: You see, the style of the Trungpas as it relates to a monastic situation and that kind of bureaucracy won't continue at this point. But the teachings of Buddhism continue to flourish in this country. Maybe the next Trungpa will be just *one* of the leaders, rather than the messiah.

S: But would he be considered a Trungpa, or would he be a—

CTR: Well, it's uncertain what kind of a name he might have. That doesn't really matter.

S: Rinpoche, could you say a little more about beginning at an ordinary level, beginning with confusion, and then clicking in to an area of sanity and cultivating that?

CTR: It's a question of how much you do, as opposed to what you just talk about doing. You can't purely talk about transforming confusion. Otherwise you might be caught up in a very powerful, slick trick, and then you are completely fooled.

S: But there's some sense that we'd better do it now?

CTR: *Right now.* Allen?

Allen Ginsberg: This is a somewhat similar question to what was raised before. Is the Trungpa lineage continuable in America, given the situation here? Would you like to see some form of that lineage continuing, and would that involve a tulku? Or is that something that is up to the sangha here to try to figure out with you?

CTR: I think it depends on how the psychology of the sangha actually evolves. The general plan is that some kind of reign of sangha-ship will take place for a while. That's how it happened at the beginning of many lineages. At the beginning, we didn't have tulkus of Naropa constantly. We had Naropa and Marpa and Milarepa and Gampopa, who were separate individuals, successive high-ranking, highly developed students. Then when the actual fermentation took place, finally they were able to reproduce their particular reincarnation, their particular teachers. It's a little tricky at this point to have a little kid on whom you lay a lot of trips. Quite possibly, that little kid might not buy it, if he's smart enough! [*Laughter*] I wouldn't buy the idea that I'm going to come back. [The implication is that the next Trungpa wouldn't believe that he actually was the Trungpa or that he was going to come back again as another Trungpa.—Ed.] [*Laughter*]

AG: Can you envision, though, students with enough energy, meditation, and prajna to continue on the level that you're working?

CTR: Yes, well, I think it needs group spirit. Quite hopefully, it has been said that the Kagyü lineage gets better as the time gets darker. The Kagyü lineage becomes much brighter.

AG: With the children stronger than the parents?

CTR: Yeah, yeah.

S: Do you think it's possible for any future Trungpas to be a woman?

CTR: That's an interesting thought. [*Laughter*]

S: Why weren't there any women in the lineage? Or were there women that we don't know about?

CTR: Well, there were a lot of them, but none of them became particularly ... men. [*Laughs; laughter*] Historically, how things developed was based on the social situation. The men were hard workers and they went out—if they had work to do. You know, Gampopa was pushed by his wife to go out and become a saint. [*Laughter*] [This remark was said in a way that implies that

Gampopa's wife wanted him to succeed at something and support the family by becoming a saint.—Ed.] In those days, there was no automation, no washing machine, no automatic babysitter, so everybody had to do everything manually and share everything on the domestic level. So I don't think the roles of men and women were a reflection of the teachings, but it was just purely a social norm. Men went out and did most of the work outside, and the women stayed back and bore the children and did domestic work. I'm sure that Milarepa's mother was a very powerful factor in Milarepa becoming Milarepa. There were a lot of women saints, women siddhas, but they were not particularly celebrated, prominent, in the lineage of the Kagyü or in many other traditions.

S: Do you think it will change in the future if the tradition continues?

CTR: Sure, hopefully. That's an interesting or auspicious ending, actually. Maybe one of the Trungpas will be a woman in the future! It will be an interesting experience. [*Laughs; laughter*] Why not? Gladly.

From an experiential view, the point here is not to speculate too much on history and which Trungpa was a good guy or a bad guy. Rather, by studying this material, we are trying to encourage the sitting practice of meditation. The future seed of the potential lineage, such as the line of the Trungpas, can be born out of your particular participation, your work. As we discussed already, it's not so much which was the good king, which was the bad king, as in generations in history. The king is also produced by the public. Of course, such a king cannot be particularly inbred. But once the king has been born, he needs to be educated properly. It depends on the general public intelligence that exists around that world, that particular area in which a king is born.

Historical studies and the scholarship of talking about the Trungpas may be futile. The question is: How can we create our next line of lineage holders, which remains sane and powerful in American Buddhism? This is entirely your responsibility, as well as mine. I'm doing my best, and you should do your best. In the meantime, keep on sitting a lot.

The Trungpa Tulkus

The following is a lightly edited transcript of the final talk Chögyam Trungpa gave at the 1974 Vajradhatu Seminary, an advanced program of study. It was given a year before the Mishap Lineage seminar ("The Line of the Trungpas") took place. It provides additional information about the fundamental concept of a tulku, as well as the Trungpa lineage specifically, so it seemed appropriate to append it here.

I WOULD LIKE TO discuss the Trungpa lineage and how the notion of tulkus fits into all of this. The tulku principle is basically connected with the three-*kaya* principle as well as the idea of the guru principle, the *yidams*, and other vajrayana principles. I think basically it is very simple. The enlightened state has three levels: the *dharmakaya*, which is the ultimate being, the origin of everything, formless and all-pervasive; the *sambhogakaya*, which is the manifestation of the activities of dharmakaya into the visible level of energy, play, and everything; and the *nirmanakaya*, which represents the sense of actual earthly connections, energy materializing on a physical plane, particularly as human beings. The good intention extends toward all the rest of the realms as well, but in general the enlightened ones find that human beings are more workable. They speak language; they have developed intelligence; they have complicated social systems; and they also experience pain more acutely than beings in the other realms, who are dissolved much more into their own confusion and so are more freaked out than human beings. So the human realm is the most workable situation of all.

The Tibetan translation of "nirmanakaya buddha" is *tulku*. *Tul* means "emanation," and *ku* means "body," so *tulku* means "emanated body." In this context, for instance, Gautama Buddha is a tulku.

There are several types of tulkus. The Buddha on earth is one type of tulku. The images of Buddha are also known as tulkus, "tulkus of art." Another tulku is the tulku who continues to be reborn constantly in order to help beings on various levels. But the Tibetan tradition of discovering tulkus who are incarnate lamas, that somebody is the tulku of so-and-so, is a different kind of setup, in a sense. There are actually various types of incarnate lamas and various types of rebirth taking place. There is the tulku who incarnates before the previous incarnation has died, several months or even years earlier. And then there is what's called a "blessed tulku," in which the previous person chooses the person who is closest to him, or blesses some passing *bodhisattva* who hasn't quite attained the highest of the *bhumis*. He blesses that person, and he takes certain types of energy, or spiritual energy, which transcends ego anyway, and transfers it to the chosen person. That person then comes back as the incarnation of the previous person. Actually it is a different kind of ego; but at the same time there is a spiritual continuity that takes place. Those are the various levels of incarnation.

Generally in Tibet the blessed tulkus seem to be most prominent. Such tulkus have to be raised and educated; they have to go through training and practice and everything. They have the element of realization; they have more potential of realization than just an ordinary person who has no push or encouragement and nothing injected into them. So these people have a great deal of potentiality. But they haven't quite realized it, so therefore they have to go through training, education, and everything. They begin to come up to the level of their previous incarnation because such spiritual energy has been put into them.

The reason why this is possible but we ordinary people can't do it is because we believe ourselves to be one entity, in spite of philosophical indoctrination. So we find it very difficult to split our personality, unless we become schizophrenic, which is the neurotic level, not a very pleasant or enlightened way of splitting oneself. So there may be a higher level of splitting personality, not into just one person, but many. Usually the body, speech, mind, quality, and action aspects of a particular being are transferred. So you have five types of tulkus, who particularly specialize in scholarship or contemplation or are very active in propagating the dharma, and so forth. So the Dalai Lama, Karmapa, or any other tulkus that we can think of seem to be generally the blessed-tulku type of personality. They are recognized by their predecessor, and that person actually blesses that new ego of somebody who is already making some progress in some way. They encourage them or enforce them in a certain way so that the person can reincarnate as the next Karmapa or the next Dalai Lama. Therefore such a person also has to study and go through various trainings. Otherwise, if everybody is already enlightened or if everybody has to begin all over again, it seems to give the wrong impression. If in each life you have to struggle all the time, it seems to contradict the perpetuating development of enlightenment.

Another question is, what happens to those people who have already injected their essence and their wisdom into somebody else? What happens to the original people? Where do they go? It seems that those original people also come back to this world, not as the reincarnation of themselves particularly, but anonymously, incognito, so to speak. They come back as farmers or fishermen or businessmen or politicians or whatever. They don't necessarily have to come back into a Buddhist environment particularly, because the teachings of enlightenment could be taught at any level. People can be helped at all kinds of levels. That seems to be the basic point. There are possibilities of meeting such people who never heard or thought about any form of the teachings of Buddha, but who somehow are realized in themselves. And in such cases some memories exist within them; they have some idea of their basic being. But there's no point in advertising that eccentricity, particularly if they're going to communicate with the ordinary world. So that seems to be the general setup.

In connection with that I was thinking of discussing some of the Trungpas, who are notable as a whole lineage of blessed incarnations. There are ten incarnated Trungpas. The first one is not an incarnation of Trungpa but Trungpa himself, which makes eleven Trungpas and ten incarnations.

The First Trungpa was one of the disciples of Trung Ma-se, a siddha who was a disciple of the Fifth Karmapa, Teshin Shekpa. Trung Ma-se was born in the far east of Tibet as a prince. He renounced his kingdom and became just a traveler. Then he arrived at Karmapa's monastery and became a disciple of the Fifth Karmapa. Karmapa sent him back to his home ground and told him to start anyplace where he could find a practicing place and a teaching situation. So he came back to East Tibet and settled down. He practiced meditation there in a hut made out of reeds. He spent a long time there doing sitting meditation practice, something like six years, and he had very little to eat, but nobody discovered who he was. Eventually he began to feel that he was able to relate with students and that he was in a situation to do so. The story says that he decided to go back and ask his guru. But somehow he got a message—some merchants brought mail for him that said something like, "Don't come back. Go ahead." He understood this to mean that he didn't have to ask if it was OK for him to teach or not. So he realized the message. Then, having gotten the message, he came back to his hut again and began to teach. In particular he began to teach the six yogas of Naropa and the teachings connected with that—anuttarayoga.[1] He was an expert on that and he gathered a large number of disciples. The local principalities also began to take an interest in his teachings and his being. He had already built the reed hut so he began to teach in that hut. Eventually he had eleven disciples. Eight of them were called the "eight realized ones," and three of them were called the "three idiots." [*Laughter*] The First Trungpa was one of the three idiots.

The word *trungpa* is an honorific term, which literally means "attendant." Ideally when somebody serves their guru twenty-four hours a day, they begin to get some glimpse of the workings of his mind. They begin to get messages and reminders of awareness and things like that. So the best way to develop is to be the guru's servant. That's the tradition. So *trung* means "close," "nearby," and *pa* makes that a noun, so *trungpa* means "he who is close to the teacher."

The First Trungpa was born in the family of one of the local lords. He was educated and raised as an educated person. In his youth, his teens, he worked with his father ruling the country, collecting taxes, and fighting with the hostile neighborhoods and everything. Then he left his kingdom, his principality. He had heard the name of Trung Ma-se, so he abandoned his home and settled with him. He spent a long time, something like twenty years, practicing meditation. And he received a lot of teachings at the beginning: the various levels of studying Chakrasamvara tantra; and various sadhanas such as the external sadhana, the internal sadhana, the secret sadhana, and so forth. He studied and practiced the six doctrines, or yogas of Naropa. And then his teacher sent the First Trungpa away. He said, "Now it is time for you to go away from me; you have received enough of what I have. You should find your own monastery, your own place to stay, and teach other people."

So he visited various places. He traveled toward East Tibet and came to the fort of Adro Shelu-bum, who was the local landowner and local lord. When the First Trungpa arrived, he was repeating a text of Manjushri [see chapter 4, note 3]. In it there's a particular phrase, *chökyi gyaltsen lekpar dzuk,* which means "Firmly plant the banner of dharma." So he arrived at the door of Adro Shelu-bum's castle with that particular verse. He was well received and he became a teacher of Adro Shelu-bum, who offered his fort and his castle as a monastery. Without very much interest, the First Trungpa accepted, but then he just continued his travels.

The Second Trungpa (there are very few stories about him) was also a traveler. After the First Trungpa's death, the Second Trungpa was discovered by Karmapa, as usually happens. The Second Trungpa was discovered as an incarnation of the First Trungpa. But there was no monastery, no establishment. He just became a student of Trung Ma-se, a student of a student of Trung Ma-se by that time.

During the time of the Third Trungpa, something happened. The Trungpa incarnations organized a group of Surmang monasteries, which were not previously actually stationed in one place. They usually camped around. In fact it was called *Surmang Garchen,* which means "Surmang, the great camp." The monks traveled in caravans: their libraries were on pack mules, the shrine was a large tent, the monks' quarters were also tents, and the abbots' quarters were tents as well. There were supposed to have been something like 140 people traveling around. They usually traveled among the different districts of East Tibet; they traveled great distances. The pattern of the culture was that you traveled in the highlands during the summer when the highlands were not too cold, and you traveled in the lowlands in winter because the climate there was relatively reasonable. And they set up temporary monasteries in each place they camped. So the monks had their practices developing, and the student newcomers could be instructed. And in many cases, local students began to join the camp; they wanted to become novices and they were accepted. So as they went on, their camp became larger. That was the pattern in Tibet at the time. Tsurphu, the Karmapas' monastery, was itself happening in that fashion. It was called the "great camp of Karmapa." So in most of Tibet, the Tibetan monastic system was not in permanent dwelling places but in tents.

Finally, at the end of the life of the Third Trungpa, one of the Karmapas (I don't remember exactly which generation of Karmapas it was) had a sudden insight. He sent an invitation to the Third Trungpa to come and visit him. So the Third Trungpa took a journey to Central Tibet, which usually takes about six months, and Karmapa told him that the prophecy of the *mahasiddha* Dombipa had come true: "It is you. You are the incarnation of Dombipa. And the prophecy goes like this. Dombipa lived in India. One evening at the end of his life he was drinking out of his skull cup, and he finally decided to transplant his mahamudra teachings somewhere other than India. He said, 'In ten lifetimes'—or something like that—'I'll be going wherever my skull cup lands.' And then he threw his skull cup into the air and the skull cup flew across India and landed in Surmang, on a particular little mountain. So you should establish a permanent monastery there." And the place where the skull cup landed happened to be the castle of Adro Shelu-bum. Since then it has been called "Dütsi Tel," *dütsi* meaning "amrita" and *tel* meaning "hill." Apart from that story about how the Third Trungpa received instructions to establish a permanent monastic residence, nothing very much is known about him.

The Fourth Trungpa was very well known as a teacher throughout the Kagyü tradition. He was the only person who actually received what's called the *"shi-je* tradition," one of the contemplative schools of Tibetan Buddhism often associated with the teachings of chö.[2] The basic philosophy of chö is that, instead of asking for protection from the Mahakalas or your guru, you give up your negativities and your security and ask the enemies or the demons, whoever they are, to consume you. That particular technique is very revealing to a lot of people, particularly in dealing with death and dealing with life, sickness, and chaos. That particular practice is actually something that the contemplative tradition extracted, so to speak, from the prajnaparamita sutras. As well there is a touch of tantric outrageousness, stepping on your problems, stepping on your threat. That particular practice is called "chö," and it usually takes place in the evening or at night.

The Fourth Trungpa made retreat centers, something like 108 retreat centers, supposedly in haunted places. And at the age of twenty-four he actually left his monastery. He bestowed the ruling of his monastery on his brother, and he traveled around the country. He had a white yak without any horns, which is the most domesticated type of yak, so that it wouldn't be temperamental. It had a ring through its nose so you could lead it wherever you wanted. He rejected any services from the monastery and decided to travel by himself. In our monastery we used to have the ring, the wooden loop, that went through his yak's nose. And he had a thighbone trumpet, which we also used to have in the treasury of the monastery. He used it to call the haunting evil spirits to eat you up.

The Fourth Trungpa was also one of the great teachers of the subsect of the Kagyü tradition called the Nedo (Tib. *gnas mdo*) Kagyü, which is not included in the four great and the eight lesser schools. It developed based on the idea of the Pure Land. Like the Pure Land tradition in Japan, it placed enormous emphasis on the worship of Amitabha and so forth.[3]

So from that time onward the Fourth Trungpa actually sat in a particular cave in Dütsi Tel—in a valley just north of Dütsi Tel he found a cave—and he sat and meditated in it for six years. According to the story, he fainted many times, but he regained consciousness and still continued to practice. He rejected any kind of hospitality from his monastery.

I think one of the outstanding aspects of the Fourth Trungpa is that he was a great scholar. He wrote a three-volume commentary on mahamudra, each volume probably having about a thousand pages in it. At that time nobody had ever written a commentary on mahamudra in the Kagyü lineage except for various manuals on visualization and other things. But this particular manual of mahamudra was straightforward; nothing else like it had ever been written. And according to the stories, one of the Karmapas was very shocked that the Fourth Trungpa could say so many things about mahamudra, a three-thousand-page book. He said, "The Fourth Trungpa's skull must be bursting," or "He must be just about to explode his skull if he has so much to say about mahamudra."

The rest of the Trungpas, apart from the eighth one, are rather mellow and seem to be very ordinary, very domesticated people. The Fifth Trungpa received an official title from the emperor of China. He was given seals and various official things, because that was the time of the Moslem invasion of Tibet. He was made into what's called a *hutoktu* [see chapter 6, note 1], which is a particular title of "royal imperial teacher" or "imperial guru," or something like that. But apart from that, there isn't very much known about him.

And I think the Seventh Trungpa actually died very young. He was about eighteen years old when he died. When he was an infant his mother accidentally dropped him on the floor, which caused a concussion in his head. And that sickness continued throughout his life. But nevertheless he was supposed to be a very bright kid. He composed a lot of poems, and if his life had been prolonged, he could have written many more. He could have become a great poet-saint, but he died at the age of eighteen.

The Eighth Trungpa is known to have been a very great artist, particularly good at painting. He had a goatee and he used to love drinking a very thick tea. And he was very kind and gentle. He spent a long time practicing meditation, something like ten years. He locked himself in the top part of his castle, which had been given to him and his lineage earlier on.

Student: You didn't say anything about the Sixth Trungpa.

Chögyam Trungpa Rinpoche: Well, there's nothing very much to say particularly.

Anyway, we used to have the Eighth Trungpa's handwriting and his calligraphy and the thangka paintings that he did. It was similar to the thangkas I've seen of the kings of Shambhala, that type.[4] He actually did little thangkas of the eighty-four siddhas. They were very beautiful Gardri school paintings and fantastic works of art. And he compiled the library of Surmang, which was destroyed at the time of the Tenth Trungpa.

The Ninth Trungpa was supposedly a very shameful person, not in the sense of being wild or anything like that, but he just spent his life sitting around outside in the sun, chatting with people and taking anise snuff. He was very peasantlike and uneducated, actually. The only thing he composed in his life was four lines of a puja-type offering to Mahakala, which we used to chant in our monastery and that doesn't say very much. He was very ordinary. I think at the time there was not very much learning or very much intellectual work going on, and there was also not very much practice going on. And he just existed. His death was supposed to be a quite interesting one. He kept saying, "Tomorrow I'm going to die. Since I'm going to die tomorrow, at least I'm going to die in a dignified way." He called his attendant to come and take off his old clothes and put on his yellow robe. Then he sat up in the cross-legged vajra posture and he was gone. This was the only testimonial that he knew what he was doing.

And then there is the Tenth Trungpa. I'm sure I don't have to tell you too much. If you like, you can read about him in *Born in Tibet*, in which there are detailed stories. He was born into the family of a local lord of the Surmang district. He won lots of court cases that had been initiated against our monastery by various Geluk monasteries in our district. They were in league with the Central Tibetan government, which actually finally invaded our monastery and sacked it, and there was a court case going on afterwards. The Tenth Trungpa was a great politician, and he was also a great scholar. He had studied with Jamgön Kongtrül the Great for a long time. Supposedly in his early life when he was with Jamgön Kongtrül, he couldn't get hold of butter to make a butter lamp, so he used incense to create a glow on the text just to be able to read a little bit. Then he would memorize what he had read.

When he meditated he sat in a meditation box, which is a traditional thing. You have a little box that you sit in; you lean back at night and sleep in it, and to get up you just lean forward. So you get up and you meditate all the time. He supposedly tied his hair to the ceiling during sitting meditation so that if he nodded off, his hair would wake him up. He did that for about six years, actually. And sometimes he found that even that wasn't effective enough, so he had stinging nettles arranged around the rim of his meditation box so that if he leaned over he would get stung. He was a very tough person, and once he set his mind to something, it never changed. And he was very much into austerity. When he was searching for his guru, he abandoned his monastery; he gave up riding on horseback, eating meat, wearing leather or animal products apart from wool, and so forth.

I think that's most of the Trungpas. As we discussed previously, all the Trungpas were blessed tulkus, blessed incarnations, rather than a one-shot deal.

Student: Who were examples of the other types of tulkus? Do we know anyone by name?

Chögyam Trungpa Rinpoche: I don't think we do. I don't think there's anybody that we can mention. But sometimes some of the actual incarnations, the direct ones, are known to be a particular person, like the great Khyentse Rinpoche, Jamyang Khyentse Wangpo. There are some extraordinary stories about such people. When they are brought up and they are something like six years old, they're very articulate. They seem to know everything. And their parents begin to feel very inferior to their kids. Their kids seem to function much better in the world than they could. They haven't been taught reading or writing, or maybe they are taught just a hint of it, but they pick it up very fast and they even correct their teachers as they go on. It's the same sort of thing as Mozart, who was supposed to be playing music when he was six years old. It's that kind of approach. Very little training is needed and you can just continue all the time, and in fact get better each time. There is a genius in the family who is a direct incarnation—which doesn't seem to be the case with any of the present incarnate lamas.

Such direct incarnations need a lot of special attention. It is interesting to see what happens when an incarnate lama who was actually assigned to be a direct incarnation rejects his life completely. I met a local king in the neighborhood next to mine. He had five sons and one of them was an incarnate lama that he didn't want to let go because he didn't want him to face hardships such as being mistreated by tutors and everything. He was held back and kept home and eventually he married. And he went completely insane. People had to restrain him to keep him from jumping out of windows and things like that. Somehow something begins to fuse when you don't meet that particular kind of karmic demand from higher authorities, so to speak, and you just turn back into a vegetable.

S: In something that I read recently that gives an account of the various Kagyü sects, it said that one of the small divisions was the Surmang Kagyü. I don't know if that is true or not. But it said that there's a separate sect, called the "Surmang Kagyü," of which the Trungpas are the head. I wonder if that's true and, if so, what characterizes this particular division of the Kagyü order.

CTR: Well, the interesting point is that the Eighth Trungpa incorporated a great deal of Nyingma teachings. His role was similar to Rangjung Dorje's role in unifying the Kagyü and Nyingma teachings.[5] The Eighth Trungpa incorporated a lot of Nyingma teachings and he actually adopted Ekajati as the protector of Surmang Monastery. Actually, the Kagyü didn't have Ekajati. [She is a Nyingma protector.—Ed.] And earlier, the Fourth Trungpa's characteristic teaching was that particular chö teaching, which made him very special. And we also have the Surmang version of the complete mandala performance of the Chakrasamvara sadhana, which was translated into a form of dance. That was the discovery of the teacher of the First Trungpa, Trung Ma-se.[6] Other characteristics of the Surmang Kagyü were that there was more research work done on the six yogas of Naropa and there were definitely more studies made on mahamudra by the Trungpas, particularly the Fourth Trungpa's commentary. Based on that, the Surmang people had a great deal of information about mahamudra. They were experts on that. And in fact the Fifteenth Karmapa actually invited Tendzin Rinpoche, who is supposed to be the previous birth of Taggie [Chögyam Trungpa's son], to teach him the Surmang Kagyü's ideas about mahamudra.

But soon after the Fifteenth Karmapa died, and Tendzin Rinpoche also died, so there was no chance to do that. So mahamudra seems to be one of the Surmang Kagyü specialities in which they are expert; another is bringing the Nyingma tradition into the Kagyü. The Tenth Trungpa was very emotional about the Nyingma tradition. He and Gyaltsap Rinpoche, who was Jamgön Kongtrül of Sechen's teacher, had sort of a spiritual love affair. The Tenth Trungpa would say, "I wish I was born in your monastery," and Gyaltsap Rinpoche would say the same to him. There was a very moving experience before the Tenth Trungpa left Sechen, where he met Gyaltsap Rinpoche. The two of them went up to the roof of the monastery, and they sat together and chanted this tune of invocation to Ekajati, so that Ekajati would keep an eye on them after they departed and they would still be together.

I think that, not in a particularly flashy or extraordinary way but in a very subtle way, the Surmang people have somehow managed to maintain their intelligence and wisdom.

S: Could you say something more about the lama dance?
CTR: It's very elaborate. It has 360 moves or themes, and the performance usually takes about a day and a half; there's about a three-hour performance first, which is the preparation of the ground; and then there is another approximately five-hour performance establishing the shrine, the creation of a mandala; and then there is a twenty-four-hour dance concerned with the actual mandala itself. There are certain movements connected with taking refuge and taking the bodhisattva vow as you chant and dance. And then there is exorcising the hostile environment and the calling upon blessings. And then you have visualizations. All of them are in the form of dance.

This particular dance is different from the basic Tibetan dance that you might see or have seen already in films, where the dancers are wearing robes. In this Chakrasamvara dance they are dressed in *heruka* costumes, with bone ornaments and crowns made out of bone, usually ivory or mule or horse bones, carved and inlaid with jewels and so forth. That's supposed to represent the various yogic exercises that have developed. This is part of hatha yoga practice, supposedly. The idea is that there is what's known as "fast dance" and "slow dance." In fast dance you're supposed to speed up the slow dance—which is competing with a cloud, you know; you are not moving at all. You know that idea. It's a complete sadhana; you begin to get into it more and more.

I started to learn when I was about sixteen. And not having had enough exercise the first three days, my whole body completely ached; I had flu and everything. And they said, "You shouldn't just lie down. You should come down and do at least three hours of practice." And I kept hanging on and finally I felt much better. I could get into the rhythm of the whole thing and the energy that exists. It's more like just movement dance, more connected with tai chi or something like that than the traditional Tibetan dance, which is jumpy and very fast. But this one is very slow and movement oriented. You have a drum in your right hand and a bell in your left hand, and you have to learn to use them properly as well. After every full beat, you ring your bell. So everybody has to be synchronized, the whole orchestra and all the dancers. And it's very defined, six of this and seven of that and then ten of that. Then the leaders of the dance make certain moves that indicate which part of our body we're going to use to begin with as a main movement. It's very much like the feeling of Chakrasamvara; you dance all the time. And you sort of put your passion out constantly. You relate with your passion. And the more you relate with your passion, the more you get into it.

This particular dance is based on a great feast. So in the middle of the dance circle there's a great feast, which is eventually distributed to everybody. And there is a blessing of the feast, visualizing yourself and the altar table with the feast as part of the great mandala as well. And you bring in the jnanasattva by a certain dance movement; usually that particular part is very slow. I was able to dance only about six times, because it happens only once every year. And I began to enjoy it more every year. I wasn't particularly approved the first year as a good dancer, but as I went on I had memorized the whole thing completely. People used to carry little books attached to their ornaments or dance costumes, but I didn't have to use that either. I was very good at it; I had become a good dancer. I was actually just about to teach it the next year at the monastery. Every six years you recruit new dance students, and you spend three months training them, teaching the movements first and the disciplines, and then the actual themes and songs and everything. I was going to teach the next year and then, thanks to Chairman Mao . . .

S: Does everybody wear the same costume?

CTR: Yes. They all wear the same costume. In a certain part of the dance, all the dancers are divided into twos, you and your partner. And the movements are the opposite. The rhythms are the same but the movements are opposite, so it is very difficult to do. That's the particular part when you visualize you and your consort.

S: Are the movements one set pattern of movements? Is it the same pattern each year?

CTR: Yeah, sure. Otherwise you couldn't learn. But the movements are very precise. I found that first you have the hassle of learning the dance and how to do the dance properly. And after that you begin to know the implications behind it. And traditionally what used to happen is that when you sounded your bell a certain way or the monk in charge of chanting sounded his bell a certain way, it was a tea sound. They brought tea around as you danced. And there's also another sound you make that's the liquor sound. So you have tea and liquor alternately. And while you dance you are actually allowed to drink some kind of beer, barley beer or chang or even *arak*, which is a more concentrated sort of thing.

S: What's the quality of memory involved in being a tulku? For example, do you have accurate, kind of acute memories of previous lifetimes?

CTR: Well, let's say that I'm not the real Trungpa, who was the tenth one, Chökyi Nyinche. I'm not him exactly, but I have maybe been part of his memory, part of his being. Goodness knows who I am—I could be a gentleman from Osaka, or one of the Trungpa's disciples, whatever. But there are memories—which it is usually forbidden to talk about for some reason. I suppose that's understandable if people are going to trip out on the whole thing. But I was only allowed to tell about memories to my tutor when I was younger. And those memories continued until I was about thirteen or something like that. It's just at the level of puberty that these memories begin to disappear. You don't get those flashback things happening anymore. Which is, I think, very significant. At the level of puberty you begin to relate with the world; you become a man of the world. Before that you are still a past-oriented infant somehow.

And I remember visiting—now I'm telling, I don't think there's any harm. There are more tutors around. [The implication here is that the author is telling these stories to tutors in the present environment, which is allowed. Normally it would be forbidden to speak of these things.—Ed.] There was a place where the Tenth Trungpa died, some local lord's house. He died in the house, and there was a particular place where his bedroom was and where the shrine and everything was. And I visited there. People were busy organizing my welcome party outside, and I was helped off my horse and walked in. Nobody was leading me. Traditionally there's somebody to lead you, you know, with incense or something, but somehow they didn't get their act together. And I had to walk in, because otherwise there'd be a lot of people waiting because it was getting rather late and everything. And as soon as I walked through the door, I knew exactly where to go and I knew where the room was. And my attendant, who had never been to the house before, followed me. All the doors were closed and he said, "Well, maybe we should get somebody." I said, "Well, let's find out first," and "How about here?" And we went on that way and everything was OK. It was exactly the same place as when the Tenth Trungpa arrived; it was arranged exactly the same way, so there was exactly the same pattern.

And another time we were lost in the rain and mist, traveling toward some nomad people with their tents set up in various camps. There's a certain fork in the road you are supposed to take. And everybody was completely bewildered and cold and freaky, and everybody was hungry. And the monk in charge of discipline with his loud voice was really getting hungry, and whenever he got hungry he got mad. Everybody was completely down. And they began to curse the people who had invited us to this strange place. I wasn't quite sure, but I thought I knew the whole way. I thought everybody knew it, you know. Then suddenly it clicked with me that nobody knew about this, but somehow I had some memory about having been here. I didn't even bother to ask the question, "Have I been here before in this life?" or whatever. Maybe when I was an infant they took me there or something. As far as I could remember, I had never been there in this body, so to speak. [*Laughter*]

There was usually a guy who rode on a white horse, who was supposed to lead the procession or journey. And then there was a guy with flags, and then a guy who carried the umbrella behind me. Then the rest of the people were supposed to follow after me; everything was set as to who comes next. Although the whole thing was very miserable, the ceremony still continued. I said that I would like to break the rule, and maybe I should go with the guy with the white horse. And my attendant didn't know what to do: "Maybe we shouldn't tell anybody. OK. Well, we should do it." And I said, "Don't tell anybody," and we broke the rule. I rode with the guy with the white horse at the head of our procession. I said, "Well, let's go this way.

Go this way and then there's going to be a pass. Then we are going to pass another village, which is not our place. We are going to pass the next one, which is not our village either. There's a bridge on the other side. Beyond that, seemingly hidden in a sort of dimple in the meadow—you can't see it until you get to it—you can see their village setup, the smoke going up and everything." And we got there. Actually I expected that somebody would be surprised about that. But nobody said anything at all. [*Laughter*]

S: Is this memory you had the same kind of memory that's operating, so to speak, from the seventh consciousness? Or is there a kind of memory that's like *bodhichitta* itself?
CTR: I really don't know, actually. I would guess that these memories seem to be based on something much purer than just the seventh consciousness, which is usually very impermanent and is liable to forgetfulness because you go through your birth and death trip, which begins to shock you so much that you forget your past constantly. That's what usually happens, basically, to ordinary people.[7]

S: Is the Trungpa line going to continue?
CTR: I don't think so.
S: You spoke of tulkus who are reborn outside of a situation where there would be Buddhist teachings, but the teachings are still in operation in their lives. But isn't there a possibility, because there's no support by having the teachings available, that these people will be prone to neuroses setting back in again? Would they forget the teachings?
CTR: I think that those people who are real incarnate persons have no problem at all, because anything that happens in their life is a reminder of their intelligence, their enlightenment, reminding them that they are completely realized beings. Nothing could undermine them at all, nothing whatsoever. I don't think there is any problem with that because they are already unconditioned in their basic being, so any condition that comes up is superfluous. The analogy is that the sun is never influenced by the clouds.

S: Do you think you're going to be a Buddhist in your next life?
CTR: I don't know.

S: Maybe?

CTR: I would be at least in essence, but who can tell?

S: So after you, there are no more Trungpa tulkus? Do you just go off somewhere and be an ordinary guy? What happens to that energy, that Trungpa tulku energy? Does that just die?

CTR: I suppose in this case, since I have no intention of continuing the Trungpa line, the energy is still there. When you give this energy to someone else, you don't give it away—you radiate it. But you have the same amount of energy left, exactly the same volume, you know. So energy is not a separate entity, particularly. A sunbeam coming through the window is not different from the sun itself.

S: So that you individually embody the Trungpa energy. It's not independent at all, but it sucks up different people at different times.

CTR: That's the idea. I was hoping to come back in Japan as a scientist.

S: Are we more likely to be reborn around you or reborn back in the sangha here? Is there a connection specifically with you?

CTR: There must be *something* happening. Maybe one of you will introduce me to *Meditation in Action* or *Cutting Through Spiritual Materialism*. And then we could work our way around.

S: Did you just recently discover that—you seemed to say before that you weren't the real Trungpa—

CTR: What?

S: You seemed to say before that you weren't the real Trungpa, that you weren't Chökyi Nyinche or something like that. And that you might have been one of his disciples, that you were involved with his energy. That was a very shocking remark to me. What did you mean by saying you weren't the real Trungpa? I'm very upset.

CTR: Well, it's saying the same thing as what we just discussed about the blessed tulkus. Since we have exposed the mystique of incarnations tonight, I thought I should make myself very articulate. Otherwise I wouldn't bother to question whether a Trungpa is real or unreal. Who cares? Even the Tenth Trungpa wasn't really "real." Or the First Trungpa wasn't real [he wasn't the same person] as soon as he became the Second. There's always duality.

S: Is there any special relationship between the teachers of the Trungpa tulkus?

CTR: I think very much, yes. It's like my relationship to Jamgön Kongtrül of Sechen. He was also the student of the Tenth Trungpa, who studied with Jamgön Kongtrül the Great as well.

S: So unique relationships exist between the teachers?

CTR: I think so. Jamgön Kongtrül of Pepung, who was my preceptor, is known to have an incarnation in Rumtek Monastery, the seat of the Karmapa. When I was at Rumtek the last time, meeting him felt very personal.[8] I paid my respects to him, and there was some feeling that continued happening from my relationship with the previous incarnation. Actually I think I frightened him when I visited him. He didn't know exactly what to do. I was coming on with strong emotion, and he was just an innocent little kid.

Light of Blessings

Supplication to the Eleventh Trungpa, Chökyi Gyatso

In supreme unchanging great bliss, vajradhatu,
Forefather who emanates and gathers all kayas and buddha fields,
Glorious heruka, lord of oceans of mandalas,
We supplicate the guru, the primordial buddha.

From the wisdom play of all-pervasive compassion,
You continually appeared as the learned and accomplished
    charioteers of the teachings
Of India and Tibet and especially of the Kagyü and Nyingma.
We supplicate you.

In particular, as the magical emanation of sacred wisdom,
Lord, your marvelous virtues of hearing, contemplating, and
    meditating
Manifested for our sake as buddha activity.
Chökyi Gyatso, we supplicate at your feet.

Actualizing the wisdom of ultimate dharmata,
Confusion exhausted at its base, your spontaneous wisdom
    came forth.
Apparent existence perfect as the one mandala of dharmakaya,
We supplicate space, Chökyi Gyatso.

By the power of birth and death being naturally pure in
   enlightenment,
With the vision of compassion beyond decrease or increase,
Looking after us disciples who are left behind,
Please ripen and free our beings.

Perfecting the excellent path of the effortless yana,
Glorious guru, may our minds mix with yours.
Thoroughly liberated in the youthful vase body endowed with
   the six qualities,
May we perfect the two benefits.

*Encouraged by gifts and the sincere mind of faith of Könchok Paldrön,
secret friend of the supreme one, Mangala Shri Bhuti [Dilgo Khyentse
Rinpoche] wrote this. May it be a cause for seeing the very face of the guru
of the ultimate natural state.*

Translated by the Nalanda Translation Committee.

Editor's Afterword

I N THIS VOLUME, Chögyam Trungpa articulates the forces and the principles that shaped the lineage of enlightened teachers and teachings from which he came, while also demonstrating how our practice and study of the teachings today is shaped by similar issues. "The Line of the Trungpas" seminar, on which most of the present volume is based, took place at the Karmê Chöling meditation center near Barnet, Vermont, in December 1975. It was an opportunity for Rinpoche to reflect back on the history of his lineage from the perspective of having been in the West for more than ten years and in North America for five years, during which time he had gathered around him a sangha of more than one thousand committed practitioners. These discussions were clearly related to how he viewed the introduction of the Buddhist teachings in North America and his hopes for their future.

When Chögyam Trungpa arrived in America in 1970, he was somewhat of a renegade, from the point of view of the Kagyü lineage. He was estranged from some Tibetan colleagues, and His Holiness the Gyalwang Karmapa, the head of the lineage, was not sure what Trungpa Rinpoche was up to. It must have been difficult for the Karmapa to fathom what Chögyam Trungpa was doing in North America. Tales of the counterculture folk who flocked to him and the lifestyle he adopted to accommodate them must have seemed questionable to the traditional Tibetan world. In 1974, Trungpa Rinpoche invited the Karmapa to visit the United States, just a few months after two thousand spiritual seekers, aka students, came to the first session of the Naropa Institute. By that time, Rinpoche had also conducted the first Vajradhatu Seminary, an advanced three-month program of practice and study, and he was in the middle of conducting a second seminary. He had more than two hundred students who were practicing or about to embark on the vajrayana practices of ngöndro. The Karmapa surely would have been somewhat surprised by the sophistication of Western practitioners, and no less by the devotional outpouring that accompanied his arrival in America. From all indications, he was delighted and moved to see that Trungpa Rinpoche was in fact pouring his heart and the lifeblood of the lineage into the American psyche and that he was succeeding admirably in "taming untamable beings."[1] In a ceremony in Boulder, Colorado, attended by hundreds of Trungpa Rinpoche's students, the Karmapa confirmed Chögyam Trungpa as a vajra master whose mission was to plant the seeds of the buddhadharma in American soil. In a few short years, Rinpoche had created a meeting point between the ancient tradition and the new reality of Buddhism in the American world. It was just after His Holiness had concluded his first visit to America that Trungpa Rinpoche closed the 1974 Vajradhatu Seminary with "The Trungpa Tulkus," a historical discussion of the lineage, which appears as the appendix in this volume. A year later he gave "The Line of the Trungpas" seminar. His Holiness's visit deepened the appreciation of tradition and devotion. Before that, it would have been much more difficult to tell these lineage stories in this intimate fashion.

In *The Mishap Lineage*, Trungpa Rinpoche focuses on some of the most important holders of the Trungpa lineage, while skipping over or largely ignoring others. This seems to be in keeping with the Tibetan histories written about the lineage. There is a great deal to say about some of the Trungpas and their contributions; there is little known about others.

Altogether, Trungpa Rinpoche's treatment of the historical facts and details in *The Mishap Lineage* is loose and often sketchy. Were he still alive at the time of the editing of this material, his editors would have had the opportunity to supplicate him to add additional material and to consult him about numerous details as well as inconsistencies. Since he is not here to address these issues, the material has been left with its ambiguities and contradictions.[2] Some of these have been documented in the notes. In the end, they do not take away from the main thread of these teachings, which is to give us insight into how the practitioners of the past built their Buddhist world, much as we are building it today.

In *The Mishap Lineage*, Rinpoche gives us many hints about why he was going about things in America in certain ways, and in places he also provides indications about how we should proceed. He describes, for example, how Trung Ma-se, the First Trungpa's root guru, was concerned not only about the current situation but also about future generations, and how he taught with both in mind. To guard against future problems, Trung Ma-se emphasized the sitting practice of meditation as the foundation of sanity for his students. This is reminiscent of concerns that Chögyam Trungpa expressed and of advice he gave his students.

There are puzzling contradictions in the various versions of the lineage stories that Chögyam Trungpa told at different times. For example, in *Born in Tibet*, Chögyam Trungpa's autobiography published in 1966, he tells the reader that the First Trungpa, Kunga Gyaltsen, was one of Trung Ma-se's eight highly realized students, who were known as the "eight mystics" or "eight tobdens" (Tib. *rtogs ldan yab gye*). However, in *The Mishap Lineage*, Trungpa Rinpoche tells us that the First Trungpa was not one of the mystics at all but rather one of Trung Ma-se's three idiots, who according to Rinpoche were actually the closest students of Trung Ma-se. In a meeting to review the manuscript, Larry Mermelstein (the director of the Nalanda Translation Committee) and I discussed this inconsistency with Khenpo Tsering from present-day Surmang. Khenpo seemed very surprised, almost shocked, that Chögyam Trungpa would say that the First Trungpa was one of the "idiots." He said that he and all the Surmang people knew which of the eight mystics the First Trungpa was, and that the First Trungpa was in fact the most realized of the tobdens. He referred to several texts that contain this information. Nevertheless, he also said that because this is what Trungpa Rinpoche told us, we should not change it in this book. By the end of our conversation, he said that maybe he would be the first Surmang person to say that Kunga Gyaltsen was one of the idiots. Then he laughed heartily. Whenever we discussed other contradictions between Trungpa Rinpoche's accounts in the West and the stories and texts from Tibet— which themselves are inconsistent—the Khenpo would always say that we should stick with whatever Trungpa Rinpoche said. This itself may be a clue to how spiritual history was traditionally told and regarded in Tibet: authenticity seems to have less to do with historical fact and more to do with the realization of the teller.

Interestingly, I think that many of Trungpa Rinpoche's students liked the idea that Kunga Gyaltsen was one of the idiots. It spoke to our frontier mentality, our individualism, and to our counterculture roots. Americans love antiheroes. More than that, it spoke to the direct relationship between the First Trungpa and his guru. As an idiot, the Trungpa was a down-to-earth disciple, a "just do it" kind of guy, to quote a favorite command from the Eleventh.

Most readers will presumably feel that only one version of the story can be correct, and other versions must be mistaken, but I think it is also possible to view them both as aspects of the truth. Chögyam Trungpa's approach was to focus on important influences on the lineage that would be helpful to his Western students, and to examine those influences through the life stories of the lineage holders. Did it matter if events were told differently from time to time? Not to the teller, seemingly, as long as the *point* of the story was clear.

A Buddhist understanding of non-ego might affect how one treats history. Grossly simplified, if we're not solid, then history is not all that solid either. However, it doesn't require a Buddhist view of egolessness to know that the view of history changes over time, depending on who the historian is, what his or her cultural framework is, what part of society one looks at, and many other factors. The story of Columbus "discovering" America that was taught in the 1950s is no longer told in this way in most schools—far from it. It's not unusual for a historian to change his or her view of history, but usually a scholar would point out how and why the interpretation has changed, based on new sources, information, or whatever it may be.

It may be that Trungpa Rinpoche misspoke in one place or the other, or that he himself had consulted different texts that had different versions of the stories. He was not able to bring any of these texts out of Tibet, so he would probably have been going purely on memory when he told these stories to his students. We simply don't know why the inconsistencies exist. However, we can say that Chögyam Trungpa was scrupulous about many details. We can only speculate as to why, as regards the stories of his ancestors, his approach was so fluid.

We do know that Chögyam Trungpa was not just concerned but consumed with how he was growing Buddhism in America and how to help it take root here. Throughout his tenure in North America, his job, shall we say, was to build a Buddhist world, a world of sanity, a world of practitioners. The stories of his forefathers were invoked to help build that world.

The first account of the Trungpa lineage that appeared in print was in *Born in Tibet*, Chögyam Trungpa's autobiography, originally published in 1966 in England. He was then a monk living in England, studying at Oxford University. He wrote the book with Esmé Cramer Roberts, an Englishwoman who volunteered to help him tell his life story. The result is a charming and proper English telling of the story. Several of Rinpoche's early students in England have reported that Mrs. Roberts simply changed certain things in *Born in Tibet* that she thought were "unseemly." I don't think the three idiots stood a chance with her. *Born in Tibet* was Chögyam Trungpa's first book published in the West. He too may have wanted the approach to be more formal for that reason. It is certainly very detailed, and an excellent accompaniment to the present volume.

In the Mishap Lineage seminar, Chögyam Trungpa was communicating an essential understanding of the lineage to his students, a view that he wanted them to have and to use, to inform their future practice and their efforts to help establish that lineage in the West. In this seminar, Rinpoche chose a very personal tone, weaving stories into the telling with a flavor like those you hear on grandfather's knee. I have tried to keep this intimate quality and to respect the sense of storytelling in the editing of the material. Some might prefer a more scholarly approach, but for me these are the best stories, the ones that stick.

With Chögyam Trungpa, any story begins in the same way, with the need for the practice of sitting meditation. We could almost say that his version of "Once upon a time" was "Once upon a meditation cushion. . . ." It's no surprise then that the first chapter of *The Mishap Lineage* is "The Practicing Lineage." Having given the reader the barest summary of the historical origins of the Kagyü lineage, he introduces the term *drubgyü*, or "Practice Lineage." From the beginning of the book, he also stresses the need for a teacher—which is hardly surprising, considering the subject matter of the whole seminar.

Another theme that recurs in this volume is the discussion of the administrative responsibilities of the Trungpas. Clearly, this was on the mind of the Eleventh Trungpa as he established scores of city and rural practice centers, not to mention numerous other institutions, such as Naropa Institute. In the book, he describes a certain amount of tension and ambivalence on the part of the early Trungpas about building permanent monastic headquarters. While he does not seem to have hesitated in his own efforts, he seems to appreciate both sides: the freedom and spontaneity of propagating dharma based on tent culture versus the power of institutions and "bricks and mortar." Tent culture was a part of the Vidyadhara's lineage that he clearly loved. Perhaps he gained some of his affection for camping during the long ten-month voyage he made on foot to escape from Tibet in 1959.

In any case, tent culture became a feature of the culture in which he presented the buddhadharma and Shambhala teachings in America. At the Rocky Mountain Dharma Center (RMDC) (now Shambhala Mountain Center [SMC]), starting in the early 1970s, a great tent city grew up each summer. Students pitched tents all over the land when they attended Rinpoche's summer seminars. To this day, in several areas of the SMC facility there are large cabin tents pitched on permanent platforms each summer. Tent culture was also a preeminent feature of the Magyal Pomra Encampment (MPE), which began at RMDC in 1978. This program still occurs each summer at SMC and at Dorje Denma Ling in Nova Scotia. Whereas at "land seminars" at RMDC and in other locations, the use of tents for housing was primarily functional—permanent housing wasn't affordable initially—at MPE tent culture is highly celebrated and very much a part of the discipline. At the beginning of the program, the camp is set up in an empty field and returns to that open, empty state at the end. A few compromises have been allowed, such as a permanent kitchen facility on the MPE grounds at Shambhala Mountain Center (as required by the health inspectors), but the principle underlying the program is to set up a great dharma encampment or living mandala in a day, from nothing, and then at the end of the program to return the land to its original state.

Although Rinpoche discusses the ambivalence of the Trungpas toward becoming administrative and political leaders and sympathizes with them, nevertheless he takes pride in the prominent role that the Trungpas played in governing their area of Tibet and the role they played in resolving disputes. He also discusses difficulties that arose between the Kagyü monasteries in East Tibet and the Central Tibetan government. He describes the negative view that some officials held of crazy wisdom people, even as it applied to his own ability to leave India and come to the West. Sharing this conflict with his students was another way in which Chögyam Trungpa demonstrated the depth of his trust in his Western disciples. Openly discussing these issues was also part of training his students to have critical intelligence and not to shy away from conflict and difficulty.

The discussion of Tibetan politics may help to demystify the spirituality of Tibet and make it apparent that one cannot use spirituality as a refuge from the politics of the world. Trungpa Rinpoche was concerned about corruption within Tibet in the first part of the twentieth century, and in a number of places in his writings, he attributes the root of the Communist invasion to the declining lack of genuine spirituality in his homeland—with great exceptions to be sure. Showing the human side of lineage politics helps to undercut our tendencies to overemphasize the magic and mystery of Tibet.

A rather shocking ambiguity that confronts the reader of *The Mishap Lineage* is the discussion in several places about whether the Trungpa lineage will continue. He says that the next Trungpa might consider being a woman, or that the next Trungpa might not accept that he was a tulku at all. In the appendix, "The Trungpa Tulkus," he's pretty clear that he doesn't think the Trungpa lineage will continue, but he'd like to come back as a Japanese scientist, which was echoed in other private discussions that some close students will remember. Nevertheless, there is a Twelfth Trungpa, Chökyi Senge, at Surmang Dütsi Tel now, and we also have the continuity of Rinpoche's family lineage, headed by Chögyam Trungpa's eldest son, Sakyong Mipham Rinpoche, who is the spiritual leader of the organizations that Chögyam Trungpa founded in the West.

After 1974–75, when these talks were given, there were many changes in how Chögyam Trungpa viewed the future of his lineage and his teachings.

The Twelfth Trungpa, Chökyi Senge, leading the Chakrasamvara dances at Surmang Dütsi Tel, 2006. Photo by Khenpo Tsering Gyurme.

In *The Mishap Lineage*, Trungpa Rinpoche is not trying to predict or solidify the future of the lineage. He seems most interested in provoking intelligence and awakening devotion, so that students can deal with both change and continuity in the lineage—from the perspective of their individual sanity and exertion. He also places a great deal of emphasis on his students feeling personally responsible for carrying the lineage forward. When asked by Allen Ginsberg about the future of the Trungpa lineage, he suggests that there will be a "reign" of sangha-ship.

In *The Mishap Lineage*, Chögyam Trungpa also discusses his own education and upbringing, especially how everything changed for him when he met Jamgön Kongtrül. The difference between imitation and emulation, which he mentions here, is directly relevant to the educational approach he took with his own students. Students of Chögyam Trungpa's teachings will recognize this theme as central to how Rinpoche presented dharma in the West: his emphasis on embodying the teachings rather than using them as credentials.

It's notable that Trungpa Rinpoche stresses the sitting practice of meditation throughout *The Mishap Lineage* and does not emphasize the vajrayana

Sakyong Mipham Rinpoche (right) with Chökyi Senge, the Twelfth Trungpa, at Surmang Dütsi Tel, 2001. Photo by Diana Church.

practices associated with the Trungpa lineage. He mentions the chö practice done by the Fourth Trungpa, but he doesn't provide much detail. Similarly, he refers to the famous text on mahamudra written by the Fourth Trungpa, but almost as an afterthought. Rinpoche also refers to the Eighth Trungpa receiving transmissions connected with *The Tibetan Book of the Dead*, and says that the Eighth Trungpa was one of the primary holders of the lineage of these teachings. He doesn't elaborate, however. In 1975, when these talks were given, it would have been premature to go into tantric ritual and doctrinal details with a public audience. As well, he never wanted to feed the tendency toward spiritual materialism and making credentials out of one's practice.

Although *The Mishap Lineage* does not emphasize the crazy wisdom aspect of his lineage, there are instances where it stands out. The first is the discussion of the Indian siddha Dombipa. Like Dombipa, Chögyam Trungpa was known for unconventional behavior, and often he put it to use in transmitting the Buddhist teachings. Many present-day Tibetan teachers refer to him as a mahasiddha. He used ordinary activities to great effect, absent the neurosis and aggression that usually accompany them. As it says in Dompipa's song, "He who knows the nature of mind, doesn't know the nature of one's confusion."

The Mishap Lineage also contains a story of the Fourth Trungpa, Kunga Namgyal, awakening from a swoon after meditating in a cave for many years. Trungpa Rinpoche writes that Kunga Namgyal's behavior changed radically after that, and that some people thought he was crazy, while others thought he was enlightened. Almost these exact words might be used in discussing events in the Vidyadhara's own life. His behavior and demeanor at times confounded and disturbed people. Yet from another point of view, not only was he greatly realized, but he was able to enlighten others on the spot with his unconventional manifestations, showing them an entirely different and authentic way of being. Like Kunga Namgyal, the Eleventh Trungpa was completely stubborn in his adherence to sanity and completely unwilling to compromise about that as the bottom line. Because of their own confusion, some who encountered him missed the point. Rinpoche always hoped that in the long run, people would get the punch line— for their own benefit, not his.

At the time of writing this afterword, more than twenty years after his death, he is still very alive in all of his students and his readers, still teasing us with mischief, still urging us on with constant mishaps, continuing to help us transform our confusion into wisdom. For this, we can be extremely grateful. And this, surely, is an inheritance we must pass on to future generations. May the Mishap Lineage raise the Victory Banner of Dharma throughout the world. May we never forget to supplicate the incomparable guru, Chökyi Gyatso,[3] the Eleventh Trungpa tulku.

Editor's Acknowledgments

THANKS TO the Shambhala Archives for the preservation of the audio record of the teachings of Chögyam Trungpa and for providing tapes and transcripts of the Mishap Lineage seminar and the talk at the 1974 Vajradhatu Seminary. The work of the original transcribers is greatly appreciated, as well as the efforts of the original editors of the talk from the Vajradhatu Seminary that appears here. In the 1990s, I worked with a group of senior students interested in learning to edit Chögyam Trungpa's lectures. The group did a first edit of the first two talks of the Karmê Chöling seminar on which much of this book is based. Another version was published in the newsletter of the Halifax Shambhala Centre, and yet another version of these two talks appears in volume 5 of *The Collected Works of Chögyam Trungpa*. I would like to thank these student editors for their contributions. Khenpo Tsering Gyurme was kind enough to be interviewed in connection with this book and also to allow reference to his talks on the Trungpa lineage. Larry Mermelstein was generous in answering many questions, contributing to the interview with Khenpo, and also deserves thanks for his comments on the manuscript and on the introduction, as well as his review of the Tibetan terms in the book. Many thanks to Scott Wellenbach for his generous help with Tibetan terms and his reading of the preface and afterword. Thank you to the Nalanda Translation Committee for the translation of the chants that appear here. And gratitude to Jules Levinson for insight into how Tibetan history may be viewed within the tradition.

Thanks to Rudy Wurlitzer and Lynn Davis for the opportunity to work on this book at their house in Cape Breton. To Jim, Jenny, and Amy the dog, thanks, love, and ruff. Thanks also to Ellen Kearney, who copyedited an earlier version of this manuscript. Both Ellen's overview and her attention to detail were very helpful. Thanks also to Cheryl Campbell, Ben Moore, and Vajradhatu Publications, who supported the original book proposal.

Thanks to Peter Turner, the president of Shambhala Publications, for seeing the wisdom of publishing this book, and to Sara Bercholz for her editorial stewardship of the manuscript.

Thanks to Ginny Lipson, Lyndon Comstock, Khenpo Tsering, and the Konchok Foundation for help in locating photographs. Thanks to Khenpo Tsering for permission to use his photograph of the Twelfth Trungpa, Gaye Carlson for her photograph of the shedra at Surmang Dütsi Tel, Martin Janowitz and the Shambhala Archives for the photograph of Chögyam Trungpa in the robes of the Tenth Trungpa, and Jane Carpenter for permission to use the Mukpo family portrait in Tibet, 2002.

Thanks to Diana J. Mukpo for continuing commitment to the publication of her husband's work. Thanks as well to Sakyong Mipham Rinpoche and all the members of the Mukpo family for their continuing support of Surmang, through the Konchok Foundation and other initiatives, as well as for ongoing support of Chögyam Trungpa's teachings and his legacy altogether. And finally, to Chögyam Trungpa himself, the embodiment of all the siddhas of the Trungpa lineage, to whom the IOU will never be repaid, gratitude for these teachings and the opportunity to work with them.

Carolyn Rose Gimian
Trident Mountain House,
Nova Scotia

Notes

Editor's Preface

1. According to *Born in Tibet*, Chögyam Trungpa was born in 1939. Later he corrected the date to 1940, the Year of the Dragon.

2. Termas, literally "treasures," are teachings—and often actual ritual objects—that Padmasambhava or other teachers are said to have concealed in various places in Tibet, to help people in future generations. Such teachings often reveal a new understanding, or wisdom, at the appropriate time. *The Tibetan Book of the Dead* is a famous example of terma. Some termas are discovered hidden in a rock in a cave or are found in a container left at the bottom of a river, or in other unusual places. Some of them are said to be hidden in the unconscious, and they arise or are discovered in the mind of a *tertön*, a teacher capable of revealing the terma. Chögyam Trungpa Rinpoche was a tertön who was able to find such mind termas or mind treasures as well as physically concealed terma. Before leaving Tibet, he discovered a number of physical termas in caves near Kyere Monastery.

3. The first to travel to Surmang was Lee Weingrad, who made his way there in 1987, the year that Chögyam Trungpa died. Lee later founded the Surmang Foundation, which has focused on health care and other humanitarian projects in the area. Following visits to Surmang by the Vidyadhara's eldest son, Sakyong Mipham Rinpoche, and Chögyam Trungpa's wife, Lady Diana Mukpo, the Konchok Foundation was established in 2001 to provide for the education of the Twelfth Trungpa, to help rebuild Surmang Dütsi Tel, and to establish a *shedra* there for the education of local monastics and other children.

4. In 2003, Karseng Rinpoche transmitted a guru yoga for the Vidyadhara, which Chögyam Trungpa wrote while still in Tibet. In 2006, Karseng Rinpoche conferred the abhisheka for an Avalokiteshvara sadhana that was received by Chögyam Trungpa Rinpoche as terma in Tibet. In future years Karseng Rinpoche

hopes to confer the transmissions for a wrathful Vajrayogini practice, a chö practice, and many other practices and texts received by Chögyam Trungpa as termas.

From Karseng Rinpoche, we also have begun to learn more about the history of Trungpa Rinpoche's activity as a tertön in Tibet. According to some sources, he began to discover terma as early as age six. In his teenage years, while practicing in caves near Kyere, he had a vision of the protector Ekajati, who appeared to him during a feast where many practitioners were present. She presented him with a small stone casket, which he placed on the shrine and which opened spontaneously within a few days. It contained a terma scroll, which he was able to decode and thus reveal a cycle of terma. Trungpa Rinpoche's tertön name was Trakthung Rigdzin Tsalchang. Rinpoche was the emanation of Nyak Jnanakumara, a direct disciple of Guru Rinpoche. Nyak Jnanakumara also manifested as the tertön Ramo Shelmen some centuries ago. The Nalanda Translation Committee, which is deeply involved in translating all the texts collected by Karseng Rinpoche, is documenting Trungpa Rinpoche's activity as a tertön in Tibet and gradually making this information available. This only deepens the appreciation of the terma that Rinpoche found in the West. Considered against the background of what he found in Tibet, his Western terma discoveries seem unquestionably genuine and more and more extraordinary.

He received three large collections of terma teachings in Tibet. Many of these were lost when the Communist Chinese took over the area, but a remarkable number have survived through Karseng Rinpoche's efforts and the steadfastness of Trungpa Rinpoche's disciples in Tibet. The three collections are the teachings of the *Embodiment of the Wisdom of the Three Roots*, the teachings of the *Profound Heart-Essence*, and the teachings of the *Heart Treasure of Samantabhadra*. For each of those three, there is the treasury of tantric teachings, the treasury of the hearing lineage of oral instructions, the treasury of the ordinary yogic applications, and the treasury of extraordinary secrets. Furthermore, for each of those four, there are many teachings of the general and the particular, the root and the branch. (This information is excerpted from *The Great Ship of Accomplishment*, a text compiled by Karseng Rinpoche for use of a master bestowing the Avalokiteshvara abhisheka. Used here by kind permission of the Nalanda Translation Committee.)

5. The teachers from Surmang and the current practitioners there set a remarkable example of devotion and dedication to Chögyam Trungpa Rinpoche and the teachings of the Trungpa lineage. They guarded these teachings throughout a terribly difficult period. Karseng Rinpoche reported to me that following the Chinese takeover, more than ten thousand people died of starvation in the Surmang area. Today there are still many reports of malnutrition. Karseng Rinpoche is the abbot of Wenchen Nunnery, where close to one hundred nuns live in extremely modest circumstances. The nuns practice principally the teachings

of Chögyam Trungpa Rinpoche, to whom they are deeply devoted. This kind of dedication is almost inconceivable in our situation of Western affluence and freedom.

OCEAN WAVES OF DEVOTION

1. The writer of this, Jamyang Chökyi Lodrö (Dzongsar Khyentse Rinpoche), was the primary incarnation of Jamyang Khyentse Wangpo the Great, and was a disciple of the Tenth Trungpa. Of the twenty-one *shlokas*, or stanzas, the first seven deal with seven of the eight predecessors of the Trungpa tulkus. Dombi Heruka was one of the eighty-four Indian mahasiddhas. Shri Simha was one of Padmasambhava's gurus. Palkyi Dorje, a chief disciple of Padmasambhava, is known for having shot King Langdarma, a Tibetan king who tried to suppress Buddhism. Truku Repa was of a Kagyü subsect at the time of Karma Pakshi, the Second Karmapa. Lhopa Gomchung was also from one of the eight lesser schools of the Kagyü. Thingma Sanggye Trak was Kagyü/Nyingma and also a local leader.

   The following ten shlokas are for previous Trungpa tulkus. Lodrö Rinchen is the siddha Trung Ma-se Togden. "Jamyang guru" refers to Jamgön Kongtrül the Great, of whom the Tenth Trungpa was a very close and significant disciple. In the following verse, Chögyam Trungpa himself is mentioned as Kunga Lekpa, the Mad Yogin of Bhutan, who was also one of his incarnations. That he is mentioned in this line instead of in a separate shloka, as with the others, is apparently to suggest a similarity in style between the two, although this was written when Trungpa Rinpoche was ten years old. The following shloka was originally written as a supplication for Trungpa Rinpoche's long life, using the name that His Holiness the Sixteenth Karmapa bestowed upon him when he was ordained. As is customary after a teacher's passing, this was modified to accord with the previous verses.

CHAPTER ONE: THE PRACTICING LINEAGE

1. Interestingly, during the Cultural Revolution in China, the same approach was taken by the Red Guards, and one finds Buddhist temples in many parts of China where the Communist Chinese lopped off the nose, mouth, or whole face of a buddha statue.
2. At the time that this seminar was presented, the use of "trip," originating with the drug culture, was a common way of referring to self-deception or delusion. The idea of "laying a trip" on someone, which the author refers to later, could also refer to imposing one's view of things onto others, as in an "ego trip."
3. The author originally said "twentieth century," but this was changed to reflect the emphasis on what's happening *now*, which was his focus.

Chapter Two: Kagyü Lineage / Mishap Lineage

1. Baba Ram Dass was an American college professor at Harvard, originally named Dr. Richard Alpert, who after experimenting with LSD and other drugs, left the university and became a Hindu practitioner, studying with various teachers in India. He was a colleague of Timothy Leary's. Ram Dass was very popular in the late '60s and the '70s, and was well known for his book *Be Here Now*. In 1974 he was invited to teach at the first session of the Naropa Institute, where he conducted an evening class that alternated with Chögyam Trungpa's class. Here, Trungpa Rinpoche characterizes Ram Dass's style of presenting himself.
2. Chögyam Trungpa used the term *hinayana* to refer to the *shravaka* and *pratyeka-buddha yanas* or traditions. It was not meant as a derogatory term.

Chapter Three: Trung Ma-se and the Three Idiots

1. This area is now the home of Surmang Namgyal Tse, the largest of the Surmang monasteries.
2. As discussed in the afterword, the First Trungpa is often named as one of the eight realized ones. See for example Chögyam Trungpa's own account in *Born in Tibet*, chapter 2, "The Founding of Surmang."
3. There are a number of other explanations for why Trung Ma-se gave the name "Surmang" to this area. However, this one was most commonly used by Chögyam Trungpa himself.
4. Trung Ma-se was also well known as a holder of an important ear-whispered or hearing lineage within the Kagyü tradition. Chögyam Trungpa gave a thorough description of this ear-whispered lineage in the article "Sacred Outlook: The Practice of Vajrayogini" in *The Heart of the Buddha*. (This can also be found in volume 3 of *The Collected Works of Chögyam Trungpa*, pages 412–41.) In preparing *The Mishap Lineage* for publication, this editor had access to transcripts of a talk given by Khenpo Tsering Gyurme on the Trungpa lineage, which included a discussion of the hearing lineage. With Khenpo Tsering's permission, some information from that talk is included here, supplemented by comments by Chögyam Trungpa. For a thorough discussion of the Vajrayogini lineage transmitted to Chögyam Trungpa Rinpoche, the reader may wish to consult "Sacred Outlook."

   Trung Ma-se was said to be an emanation of Tilopa. In "Sacred Outlook" Trungpa Rinpoche says:

   > After studying the basic Buddhist teachings for many years, Tilopa (998–1069 CE) traveled to Uddiyana, the home of the dakinis, or female yidams, to seek vajrayana transmission. He gained entrance to the palace of the dakinis and received direct instruction there from Vajrayogini herself, who manifested to him as the great queen of the dakinis. It may be rather per-

plexing to speak of encountering Vajrayogini in anthropomorphic form.
. . . However, this account of Tilopa's meeting is the traditional story of
his encounter with the direct energy and power of Vajrayogini. (Chögyam
Trungpa, *The Collected Works of Chögyam Trungpa*, Vol. 3 [Boston: Shambhala, 2004], p. 424.)

Tilopa returned to India, where he had many disciples, primary among
them Naropa, to whom he passed on the oral tradition of the Vajrayogini and
Chakrasamvara practice, which is also called the "hearing lineage of teachings."
The Vidyadhara tells the rest of the story in this way:

The First Trungpa was a close student of the siddha Trung Ma-se (fifteenth century), who was a close disciple of the Fifth Karmapa, Teshin
Shekpa (1384–1415). When Naropa transmitted the teachings of Vajrayogini to Marpa, he told him that these teachings should be kept as a transmission from one teacher to one student for thirteen generations, and then
they could be propagated to others. This transmission is called *chig gyü*, the
"single lineage" or "single thread" transmission. Because of this, the Kagyü
lineage is frequently called the "hearing lineage." Trung Ma-se received
the complete teachings on Vajrayogini, Chakrasamvara, and Four-Armed
Mahakala, and these became the special transmission that he was to hold.
Since Trung Ma-se belonged to the thirteenth generation, he became the
first guru to transmit this particular lineage of mahamudra teachings to
more than a single dharma successor, and in fact he taught it widely. The
First Trungpa, Kunga Gyaltsen, was one of Trung Ma-se's disciples who
received this transmission. As the Eleventh Trungpa Tulku, I received the
Vajrayogini transmission from Rölpa Dorje, the regent abbot of Surmang
and one of my main tutors. (ibid., pp. 426–27)

The Surmang hearing lineage came to be regarded as a special lineage or tradition within the Kagyü lineage altogether. Chögyam Trungpa transmitted the
Vajrayogini and Chakrasamvara sadhanas to his Western vajrayana students.
Students in the West thus have the opportunity and burden of helping to preserve aspects of this tradition, as uniquely articulated by Trungpa Rinpoche. He
gave many talks to his vajrayana students, including fourteen Vajra Assemblies,
as well as many lectures to Vajrayogini practitioners, which may come to be
recognized as related to the hearing lineage. The incredibly direct understanding that he transmitted is unusual and undeniably profound. He transmitted
pith understandings that are so intimate one does feel as though they should
be whispered into the ears of practitioners, so that they travel directly to the
heart.

5. According to Khenpo Tsering Gyurme of Surmang, the family lineage did continue for a while, and then in the fifth generation became a tulku lineage as recognized by the Karmapa.

6. *Ja* was a title for the leader of two or three villages. It later became a family name. The word literally means "idiot" or "moron."

7. The Divine Light Mission was founded by Shri Hans Ji Maharaj in northern India in 1960. It was a popular movement in American spirituality in the '70s mainly due to the popularity of Guru Maharaji. Chögyam Trungpa here is referring to a heavy-handed approach to converting people to a spiritual movement or teaching.

CHAPTER FOUR: TENT CULTURE

1. At that time, Trung Ma-se had established the area around Surmang Namgyal Tse as his seat. According to Khenpo Tsering, Trung Ma-se sent the First Trungpa out to establish his own monastic seat.

2. According to Khenpo Tsering, it was Trung Ma-se who threw the cup, and it was a skull cup. In "The Trungpa Tulkus," included here as an appendix, Chögyam Trungpa tells this story in connection with the Third Trungpa. In this telling, the Indian siddha Dombipa had thrown the skull cup of liquor many centuries before, and the Karmapa recounts this story to the Third Trungpa, telling him to build his monastery wherever Dombipa's cup fell. In *Born in Tibet* Trungpa Rinpoche offers another account, in which Trung Ma-se appears to the First Trungpa in a dream and tells Trung Ma-se that he is an incarnation of the siddha Dombipa and that, just like Dombipa, he should throw a cup in the air and see where it lands. In all tellings, the cup lands on Adro Shelu-bum's roof and it is here that Surmang Dütsi Tel is eventually established.

3. In "The Trungpa Tulkus," it is the First Trungpa who is reciting the sutra. In *Born in Tibet*, it is Trung Ma-se who recites this line from the sutra *Manjushri-nama-sangiti* (*Chanting the Names of Manjushri*), VIII:28, last line, and it is in connection with the founding of Surmang Namgyal Tse. This is similar to the version of the story that Khenpo Tsering told this editor. In Khenpo's telling, a farmer is reciting the sutra, and Trung Ma-se feels it is very auspicious and must indicate that he is close to finding the place where he should establish the monastery.

4. Originally, Chögyam Trungpa referred to "Naropa Institute," which has now been renamed "Naropa University."

5. According to Khenpo Tsering, the cup that flew through the air was a skull cup, and when they found it on Adro Shelu-bum's roof, the amrita in it was boiling. This impressed everyone greatly.

6. Steve Gaskin was a counterculture hippie icon of the 1960s who traveled across the United States in 1970 with a caravan of sixty vehicles, journeying from San Francisco to Tennessee, where he and his followers founded an intentional community called "The Farm."

7. In "The Trungpa Tulkus," which appears here as an appendix, it is the Third

Trungpa who establishes the great camp of Surmang. However, *Born in Tibet* agrees with the telling in this chapter.

8. The sense here is that if one knows the nature of mind, one does not experience confusion at all.

CHAPTER FIVE: THE FOURTH TRUNGPA

1. Chögyam Trungpa did not discuss the Second and Third Trungpas in this seminar. He mentions the Second Trungpa in the appendix but doesn't say much about him. In that talk, he also connects the Third Trungpa with the founding of the great camps of Surmang and ascribes the story of throwing the cup of amrita to the Third, rather than to Trung Ma-se or the First Trungpa.

2. The author originally said "fortress nest." The garuda is a bird; this seems to be an allusion to the fortress being the home of the garuda.

3. According to Khenpo Tsering Gyurme, when Kunga Namgyal came out of this retreat, he flew down from his retreat place to the courtyard of the monastery and left his footprints in the stone. They are still there, and can be seen to this day.

CHAPTER SIX: TRUNGPAS FIVE THROUGH TEN

1. This is a Mongolian title for a spiritual teacher. *Hutoktu* is commonly cited as *khutuktu*, which comes from the Mongolian *gutuytu*. In Tibetan, the word is 'phags pa, which is the translation of the Sanskrit *arya*, or "noble one." In the standard Khalkha dialect, it is *hutagt*, which is often used as an honorific title for tulkus in Mongolia.

2. Following Chögyam Trungpa's death, the seals were placed in the Shambhala Archives in Halifax, Nova Scotia.

3. In *Born in Tibet*, this story is attributed to the Seventh Trungpa. That seems unlikely, since he died at a very young age. Esmé Cramer Roberts, the editor of *Born in Tibet*, would not have known this.

4. Chetsang Rinpoche was one of the eight *tobdens* ("mystics," "realized ones") who were students of Trung Ma-se. This particular Chetsang Rinpoche, the Sixth, was a very famous teacher.

5. In *The Hidden History of the Tibetan Book of the Dead* by Bryan J. Cuevas, in the chapter on "Traditions in Eastern Tibet," the author mentions the role of the Trungpas in the transmission of the teachings from the *The Tibetan Book of the Dead*. According to Cuevas, in Khenchen Palden Sherab Rinpoche's commentary on the Zhi-Khro of Karma Lingpa, he mentions that the grandson of Karma Lingpa, Namka Chöki Gyamtso, presented these teachings from *The Tibetan Book of the Dead* to another famous tertön, Ena Lingpa, and from him the teachings spread to Surmang. Further information about the connection of

the Surmang lineages to these teachings will no doubt come from inquiries to Karseng Rinpoche and other current teachers at Surmang.

6. According to the Khenpo Tsering, the court case was in Rashul, which is closer to Surmang than Jyekundo.

7. The king of Lhathok also gave Kyere Monastery to Surmang, which became one of the Surmang monasteries. Before his escape to India, Chögyam Trungpa resettled his family there in the late 1950s, thinking they would be safer there than at Dütsi Tel. This proved to be true.

CHAPTER SEVEN: THE ELEVENTH TRUNGPA

1. The author originally said the thirty-eighth year. This has been changed to reflect the most recent information about his year of birth.

2. The details are spelled out in the first chapter of *Born in Tibet*.

3. The questioner is referring to the final talk in the "Tibetan Buddhist Path" course taught by Chögyam Trungpa at Naropa Institute in the summer of 1974. These talks are available as a DVD series from www.shambhalashop.com.

APPENDIX: THE TRUNGPA TULKUS

1. See chapter 2, note 4, concerning the hearing lineage that Trung Ma-se held.

2. The Fourth Trungpa composed a text for the practice of chö that has remained the most important such text in the Karma Kagyü tradition, the practice sometimes being known as the "Surmang chö."

3. Karma Chagme is regarded as the founder of the Nedo Kagyü. He was an important disciple of the Fourth Trungpa.

4. Chögyam Trungpa is probably referring here to thangkas of the kings of Shambhala that are now housed in the Museum of Fine Arts in Boston. From remarks on an audiotape in the Shambhala Archives, this editor believes that students of Chögyam Trungpa had obtained slides of these thangkas, which were shown to students at the 1974 Vajradhatu Seminary. At this time, Chögyam Trungpa and a group of his students were preparing an exhibition that took place the next year at the Hayden Gallery of MIT.

5. Karmapa Rangjung Dorje introduced a high level of intellectual understanding as part of the practice, and unified the traditional mahamudra teachings of the Kagyü with the ati or *dzogchen* teachings, which until his time had been transmitted mainly through the Nyingma lineages.

6. According to information from Khenpo Tsering, the First Trungpa received the transmission of these dances directly from Chakrasamvara and Vajrayogini. As Khenpo Tsering tells the story:

> One time, the First Trungpa wanted to practice Chakrasamvara in semi-retreat and he told his students, "Seal the door; close the door, and I'm going to do this practice in here and no matter what happens, don't open

it. No matter what you hear, no matter what goes on, don't open the door." So they did that; they closed the door. He had said, "Until I tell you, don't open it." But then all kinds of noise and commotion was going on inside as if there were a big crowd in there, even though he was locked in there by himself, alone. Finally the caretaker of the retreat couldn't stand it anymore. He thought to himself, "What's going on? Something is going on in there and I have to look." So he opened the door a crack, and inside he saw Chakrasamvara and Vajrayogini and other yidams all dancing. As soon as he saw them, they vanished. They disappeared and then there was only Kunga Gyaltsen, who manifested in a very angry, wrathful way, saying, "What have you done? I told you not to open the door no matter what you heard and now you've opened the door and made this big obstacle for the dharma." The attendant whimpered and cried. Then Kunga Gyaltsen said, "Well, maybe it's OK. I got one day of this training of the Chakrasamvara dances. It would have been seven days, but perhaps this transmission of one day of the Chakrasamvara dancing will be good enough." (From an interview with Khenpo Tsering Gyurme conducted by Carolyn Rose Gimian, 2006.)

According to Khenpo Tsering, the Chakrasamvara dances are still performed every year at Surmang Dütsi Tel. Even within the small retreat center there, Dorje Khyung Dzong, they have a performance every year before the Tibetan New Year. In 1975, when the Mishap Lineage seminar was given, it's doubtful that Chögyam Trungpa knew that this tradition had survived. He would not have been able to teach the dances directly to his students in the West, because he was partially crippled on the left side from a car accident in England. However, he incorporated some of the principles of the dance into the Mudra theater group exercises that he created in the early 1970s.

7. The eight types of consciousness are the six sense consciousnesses—the traditional five senses plus mind as a sense consciousness—and then *klishta-manas*, the seventh consciousness, and the *alaya*, or eighth consciousness. At the first Vajradhatu Seminary in 1973, Chögyam Trungpa attempted to relate these terms to more well-known Western psychological ideas about mind, describing the seventh consciousness as the subconscious and the eighth as the unconscious. In that talk, he says that memory is in the seventh consciousness. Here in the appendix, however, the questioner is asking about a memory that carries over from one life to the next.

8. When this remark was made, Chögyam Trungpa had last visited Rumtek around 1968, which was during the time he lived in England.

EDITOR'S AFTERWORD

1. Taken from a longevity supplication composed by Dilgo Khyentse Rinpoche, that was a daily chant in Chögyam Trungpa's community during his lifetime.

The whole chant can be found on pages v and vi of *The Collected Works of Chögyam Trungpa,* volume 1.

2. Initially, this editor thought that she could resolve the inconsistencies, but the more they were looked into, the more contradictions and competing versions emerged. Perhaps directly consulting the various Tibetan texts that present the history of the lineage will enable future scholars to resolve the difficulties. However, the various informants I consulted told me that even the texts do not agree on all points, and the oral histories that have been passed on have different versions of certain stories.

3. *Chökyi Gyatso* is the expanded form of *Chögyam.* It means "Dharma Ocean."

Glossary

The definitions given here are based on the usage of the terms in the text and do not attempt to be comprehensive.

abhisheka (Skt., "anointment"): A ceremony, or formal experience, of vajrayana transmission. The student is ritually introduced into a mandala of a particular tantric deity, or yidam, by a tantric master and is thus empowered to visualize and invoke that particular deity. The essential element of abhisheka is a meeting of minds between teacher and student.

alaya (Skt.): The fundamental unbiased ground of mind. Also used to refer to the eighth level of consciousness, literally the "storehouse" consciousness. In that usage, it is the fundamental ground of dualistic mind and contains within it the seeds of all experience.

Amitabha (Skt.): An important mahayana and tantric deity connected with the Pure Land schools of Buddhism. Amitabha is the ruler of the western paradise, Sukhavati, and the buddha of the padma family, connected with the western quarter of a tantric mandala.

amrita (Skt., "deathless;" Tib., *dütsi*): Consecrated liquor used in vajrayana meditation practices. More generally, spiritual intoxication.

anuttarayoga (Skt.): The highest of the four tantric yanas ("vehicles"), according to the New Translation school of Marpa and his contemporaries. The first three yanas are kriya, upa, and yoga. The realization of mahamudra is the highest attainment of anuttarayoga.

asura (Skt.): A jealous god in one of the six realms of existence.

ati (Skt., also *maha ati*; Tib., *dzogchen*): Great perfection. The ultimate teaching of the Nyingma school of Tibetan Buddhism, maha ati is considered the final fruition of the vajrayana path. It teaches the indivisibility of space and wisdom. Chögyam Trungpa frequently used the term *maha ati*. The more commonly used term is now *dzogchen*.

Avalokiteshvara (Skt.): The great bodhisattva of compassion; he is an emanation of the buddha Amitabha. His limitless compassion is said to help all beings who turn to him in difficult times. His Holiness the Karmapa is considered to be an emanation of Avalokiteshvara.

bhumi (Skt., literally, "land"): One of the ten stages, or spiritual levels, that a bodhisattva must go through to attain buddhahood: (1) very joyful, (2) stainless, (3) luminous, (4) radiant, (5) difficult to conquer, (6) face-to-face, (7) far-going, (8) immovable, (9) having good intellect, and (10) cloud of dharma.

bodhichitta (Skt.): Awakened mind or heart. Ultimate or absolute bodhichitta is the union of emptiness and compassion, the essential nature of awakened mind. Relative bodhichitta is the tenderness arising from a glimpse of ultimate bodhichitta that inspires one to work for the benefit of others.

bodhisattva (Skt., literally, an "awake being"): A bodhisattva is an individual who, by taking the bodhisattva vow, is committed to helping others and who gives up personal satisfaction for the goal of relieving the suffering of others. In the Buddhist teachings, a bodhisattva is more specifically one who has committed to practicing the six paramitas, or the transcendent virtues, of generosity, discipline, patience, exertion, meditation, and knowledge.

bodhisattva vow: See **bodhisattva**.

Bön (Tib., also Pön): The pre-Buddhist religion of Tibet.

buddha (Skt., literally, "awake"): When capitalized, refers to the historical buddha Siddhartha, the founder of Buddhism, the "Awakened One." When lowercase, refers to the basic quality of wakefulness, or enlightenment; or it may refer to one of many buddhas or awakened beings who, according to the vajrayana teachings, may exist in the past, present, or future in this world or in another realm.

buddhadharma: The teachings of the Buddha, or the truth taught by the Buddha. See also **dharma**.

Chakrasamvara (Skt., literally, "binder of the net of dakinis"): An important deity in the anuttarayoga tantras and in the Karma Kagyü school of Buddhism. Vajrayogini is his consort, and in tantric iconography he is frequently shown in union with her. The Trungpas are holders of an important hearing, or ear-whispered, lineage of teachings connected with Chakrasamvara.

chö (Tib.): Tantric teachings in which the practitioner visualizes giving his body to ghosts and various spirits as an offering. Often practiced in graveyards and places that are believed to be haunted. An advanced practice for the realization of egolessness, based on applying the teachings of the prajnaparamita. The Fourth Trungpa was a great practitioner of chö and the practice he composed is still used by many practitioners today.

crazy wisdom: Meditative realization or insight that is both knowledgeable and fearless. It involves a willingness to do whatever is required in a situation in order to promote wakefulness, compassion, and sanity in the environment. The wisdom arises first; the "craziness," or unconventionality, is an ornament, or later evolution of skillful means that works together with the wisdom.

dakini (Skt.; Tib., *khandroma*): A wrathful or semiwrathful female deity signifying compassion, emptiness, and transcendental knowledge. The dakinis are tricky and playful, representing the basic space of fertility out of which the play of samsara and nirvana arises. More generally, a dakini can be a type of messenger or protector.

Dalai Lama, His Holiness the Fourteenth: Revered by the Tibetan people, the spiritual head of the Gelukpa school of Tibetan Buddhism, and the head of state of the Tibetan government in exile. The Dalai Lama is a much beloved world figure who received the Nobel Peace Prize.

dark age: In Sanskrit, this is the Kali Yuga, or the "age of vice." It refers to a time when the ethics and the aspirations of society degenerate, and spiritual teachings are difficult to practice and in danger of being lost. Chögyam Trungpa sometimes referred to the current era as the dark age, particularly in connection with the problems of spiritual materialism.

deva (Skt.): celestial being or god.

dharma (Skt., literally, "truth," "norm," "phenomenon," or "law"): Often used to refer to the teachings of the Buddha, which are also called the buddhadharma. May also refer to the basic manifestation of reality or to the elements of phenomenal existence.

dharmakaya (Skt.): One of the three bodies of enlightenment. See also **kaya.**

Dombipa: One of the eighty-four mahasiddhas of India. The Trungpa tulkus are considered to be emanations of Dombipa, a king of Magadha who became a highly realized siddha. Sometimes referred to as Dombi Heruka.

dream yoga: An advanced tantric practice in which the practitioner is aware while dreaming and able to transform the confused experiences of the dream into wakefulness. Also associated with recognizing that this life is fundamentally a dream.

dzogchen (Tib.): See **ati**.

Ekajati: A female protector associated with the Nyingma lineage, but also adopted by others, including the line of the Trungpas. Ekajati has one eye, one fang, and one breast. She was a very important protector for Chögyam Trungpa and is associated with the terma, or treasure, teachings that he received before leaving Tibet. In the West, he wrote poetry to her, painted a thangka of her, and composed a chant that is used by his students to ask her to protect the teachings.

Gampopa: Founder of the monastic order of the Kagyü lineage, Gampopa was the chief disciple of Milarepa and the author of *The Jewel Ornament of Liberation*.

garuda: A mythical bird associated with tremendous speed and power. Like the phoenix, it is said to arise from the ashes of its own destruction; thus it has an indestructible quality.

Gautauma Buddha: The historical buddha of this age or era. See also **buddha**.

Geluk: The most recent of the four major schools of Tibetan Buddhism, founded early in the fifteenth century by Lobsang Tragpa, surnamed Tsongkhapa. In this school great emphasis is placed on scriptural study and learning generally. The Dalai Lama is the spiritual head of this school. A follower of this school is called a Gelukpa.

guru (Skt.; Tib. *lama*): A master or teacher, especially in the tantric or vajrayana tradition of Buddhism.

Guru Rinpoche: "Precious Teacher," the name by which Padmasambhava, a great teacher who helped to bring Buddhism to Tibet, is often referred to by the Tibetan people. See also **Padmasambhava.**

heruka (Tib.; Skt., *daka*): A wrathful male deity in vajrayana Buddhism.

hinayana (Skt., literally, "small way"): The narrow way or path. The first of the three yanas of Tibetan Buddhism, the hinayana focuses on meditation practice and discipline, individual liberation, and not causing harm to others. The hinayana is made up of the shravakayana (the path of those who hear the dharma) and the pratyekabud-dhayana (the path of those who are individual or solitary sages). See also **yana.**

Jamgön Kongtrül of Sechen (1901–60 C.E.): Chögyam Trungpa's root teacher, one of the five incarnations of Jamgön Kongtrül the Great. Chögyam Trungpa described him as "a big jolly man, friendly to all without distinction of rank, very generous and with a great sense of humor combined with deep understanding; he was always sym-pathetic to the troubles of others."

Jamgön Kongtrül the Great (1813–99 C.E.): One of the principal teachers of nine-teenth-century Tibet, the author of the hundreds of texts and compilations of prac-tices, including a commentary on slogan practice, entitled *The Basic Path toward Enlightenment.* Jamgön Kongtrül was a leader in the religious reform movement called Ri-me that sought to discourage sectarianism and encourage meditation prac-tice and the application of Buddhist principles in everyday life.

jnanasattva (Skt.): The wisdom, or ultimate aspect, of a deity visualized in vajrayana practice.

Kagyü: Tibetan for hearing (ear-whispered), or command, lineage. "Ka" refers to the oral instructions of the teacher. The Kagyü is one of the four primary lineages of Tibetan Buddhism. The Kagyü teachings were brought from India to Tibet by Marpa the Translator in the eleventh century. The Karma Kagyü is a main subdivision of the Kagyü lineage, or school of Buddhism, which was founded by Tüsum Khyenpa, the first Karmapa, or head of the Karma Kagyü lineage. Chögyam Trungpa was a major teacher in the Karma Kagyü school of Tibetan Buddhism. The Surmang Kagyu refers to a subsect of the Karma Kagyü, which emphasizes the special instructions and prac-tices that have been initiated, incorporated, or preserved by the great teachers at the Surmang monasteries, principally the Trungpas. The Nedo Kagyü is a subsect that places great emphasis on Pure Land teachings and the visualization of Amitabha.

karma (Skt.): Deed or action. The universal law of cause and effect.

Karmapa: His Holiness the Karmapa is the head of the Karma Kagyü school, or lineage, of Tibetan Buddhism, to which Chögyam Trungpa also belonged. Karmapa means "the accomplisher of buddha activity," or enlightened activity and manifes-tation. The Karmapa is often called the *Gyalwa* Karmapa, which means "Victo-rious One;" also the *Gyalwang* Karmapa, which means "Lord of the Victorious Ones." The Sixteenth Karmapa, Rangjung Rigpe Dorje, enthroned the author as the Eleventh Trungpa when he was a young child. The Karmapa, like Chögyam Trungpa, escaped from Tibet in 1959. He established his new seat, Rumtek Monas-tery, in Sikkim. He traveled to North America three times, sponsored by Vajradhatu (Chögyam Trungpa's Buddhist organization) and Karma Triyana Dharmachakra (a

Kagyü monastery in Woodstock, New York), in 1974, 1976–77, and 1980. His Holiness passed away from complications of cancer in November 1981. His Holiness the Seventeenth Karmapa, Orgyen Trinley Dorje, made his first visit to the United States in 2008.

kaya (Skt., literally, "body"): According to tradition, the *trikaya,* or the three bodies of enlightenment, refers to the three modes of existence of the Buddha, or enlightenment itself. These correspond to mind, speech, and body. The *dharmakaya* (dharma body) is unoriginated, primordial mind, devoid of concept. The *sambhogakaya* (enjoyment body) is its environment of compassion and communication. The *nirmanakaya* (emanation body) is the buddha that takes human form. In the mahayana, this usually refers to Shakyamuni, the historical buddha; in the vajrayana, it may refer to the body, speech, and mind of the guru.

lama (Tib.; Skt., *guru*): A title for a Tibetan teacher of dharma. The title can be used as an honorific title conferred on a monk, nun, or advanced tantric practitioner to designate a level of spiritual attainment and authority to teach it; or it may be part of a title such as Dalai Lama or Panchen Lama, applied to a lineage of reincarnate teachers. See also **guru.**

lama dance: A generic or popular term to refer to dances with spiritual significance done by monastic practitioners in Tibetan monasteries. Chögyam Trungpa was highly trained in the Chakrasamvara dances done each year at Surmang, a form of "lama dance."

Mahakala (Skt.): The chief dharmapala, or protector of the dharma. He is wrathful and usually depicted as either black or dark blue. The Four-Armed Mahakala is one of the chief protectors of the Surmang monasteries and of the Trungpa lineage.

mahamudra (Skt., literally, "great symbol" or "seal"): The central meditative transmission of the Kagyü lineage. The inherent clarity and wakefulness of mind, which is both vivid and empty.

mahasiddha (Skt.): A greatly accomplished practitioner and wise teacher in the vajrayana tradition who has accomplished siddhi, or great power. Often used in reference to teachers who are unconventional, nonmonastic masters of meditative realization. See also **siddha.**

mahayana (Skt., literally "great vehicle"): The second of the three yanas of Tibetan Buddhism, the mahayana is also called the "open path" or the "path of the bodhisattva." Mahayana presents a vision based on shunyata (emptiness), compassion, and the acknowledgment of universal buddha nature. The mahayana path begins when one discovers bodhichitta in oneself and vows to develop it in order to benefit others.

The path proceeds by cultivating absolute and relative bodhichitta. The result is full awakening. The ideal figure of the mahayana is the bodhisattva who is fully awake and who works for the benefit of all beings.

Maitreya (Skt.): The future or coming buddha, the buddha of the next era. See also **buddha.**

maitri (Skt.): Loving kindness, which together with compassion, or *karuna*, constitutes the activity of a bodhisattva.

mala (Skt.): Similar to a rosary in the Catholic tradition. A mala is a strand of 108 beads that is used for counting repetitions of mantras or other chants.

mandala (Skt.): A total vision that unifies the seeming complexity and chaos of experience into a simple pattern and natural hierarchy. The Tibetan word *khyil-khor*, used to translate the Sanskrit term, literally means "center and fringe." A mandala is usually represented two-dimensionally as a four-sided diagram with a central deity, a personification of the basic sanity of buddha nature. Three-dimensionally, it is a palace with a center and four gates in the cardinal directions. Mandala may also relate to the gathering of vajrayana practitioners to invoke the mandala of a particular yidam.

Manjushri (Skt.): Bodhisattva of knowledge and learning who is connected with the development of prajna, or intellect, and jnana, or wisdom. Usually depicted with a book in his left hand and the sword of prajna in his right hand. Alternatively, he may be holding a vase containing the treasure of the dharma in his left hand.

Marpa (1012–97 C.E.): The third of the great Kagyü lineage holders, and chief disciple of Naropa. Known as Marpa the Translator, Marpa was the first Tibetan in this lineage, and introduced many important teachings from India into Tibet.

Milarepa (1040–1123 C.E.): The most famous of all Tibetan poets and quintessential wandering yogin, Milarepa, or the "cotton-clad Mila," was Marpa's chief student and the fourth major lineage holder of the Kagyü tradition. His songs of realization are still recited and studied.

Naropa (1016–1100 C.E.): A great Indian siddha, or tantric master; the second of the enlightened lineage of teachers of the Kagyü lineage of Tibetan Buddhism. Naropa was a greatly accomplished scholar at Nalanda University; he left Nalanda when he realized that he understood the literal meaning of the teachings, but not their true sense. He underwent many trials before he attained enlightenment. Chögyam Trungpa gave a number of seminars on Naropa's life and teachings, several of which are published in his book *Illusion's Game: The Life and Teachings of Naropa.*

ngöndro (Tib.): the preliminary, preparatory, or foundational practices common to all four schools of Tibetan Buddhism. The preliminary practices establish the foundation for more advanced practice.

nirmanakaya (Skt.): "Emanation body," "form-body," or "body of manifestation." Communication of awakened mind through form, specifically, through embodiment as a human being. See also **kaya.**

nonmeditation: One of the four stages, or yogas, of mahamudra, in which the differentiation between meditation and ordinary experience dissolves.

Nyingma: The oldest of the four major schools of Tibetan Buddhism. Padmasambhava is the founder of the Nyingma school. See also **Padmasambhava** and **Guru Rinpoche**.

Padmasambhava: One of the eight aspects of Guru Rinpoche, a great teacher who helped to bring Buddhism to Tibet from India in the eighth century. He is considered the father of Buddhism in Tibet and is revered by all Tibetan Buddhists, but his teachings are primarily associated with the Nyingma lineage. He hid many teachings, which are called terma, in various places in Tibet, to be discovered for the use of future practitioners. See also **Guru Rinpoche**.

prajna (Skt.): "Transcendent knowledge" or "perfect knowledge," it is the sixth paramita. It is called "transcendent" because it sees through the veils of dualistic confusion. Prajna is like the eyes and the other five paramitas are like the limbs of bodhisattva activity. Prajna can also mean wisdom, understanding, or discrimination. At its most developed level it means seeing things as they are from a nondualistic point of view.

prajnaparamita (Skt.): The paramita, or mahayana practice, of prajna, or discriminating awareness. When capitalized, the term *Prajnaparamita* refers to a series of about forty mahayana sutras, which were gathered together under this name because they all deal with the realization of prajna. See also **prajna.**

prana, nadi, and bindu (Skt.): Prana relates to the wind, or movement, of mind; nadi relates to the channels in the body and in the world, through which prana moves; and bindu refers to the substance, or seed, of mind itself. They relate to tantric practices in both the mahamudra and the ati traditions.

puja (Skt.): Ritual and often devotional practice that may include bowing, prostrations, and chanting.

sadhana (Skt.): A ritual text, as well as the accompanying practice. Ranging from very simple to more elaborate versions, sadhanas engage the mind through meditation, the body through gestures (mudras), and the speech through mantra recitation.

Sakya: One of the four major schools, or lineages, of Tibetan Buddhism, known for a balance of scholarship, meditation, and contemplative studies.

sambhogakaya (Skt.): "Body of enjoyment," or "energy." The environment of compassion and communication linking the dharmakaya and the nirmanakaya. See also **kaya**.

samyag-jnana (Skt., literally, "excellent wisdom," "right wisdom," or "perfect wisdom.")

sangha (Skt.): The third of the three objects of refuge (buddha, dharma, sangha). In a narrow sense *sangha* refers to Buddhist monks and nuns; in the mahayana sense, the word refers to the entire body of practitioners, both lay and monastic.

shamatha-vipashyana (Skt.): The combination of mindfulness and awareness, principally in the sitting practice of meditation.

Shambhala: A mythical kingdom in which Shakyamuni Buddha is said to have taught the *Kalachakra Tantra*. Chögyam Trungpa presented a series of teachings on basic goodness and human warriorship, using the image of the Shambhala kingdom as an enlightened society.

shedra (Tib.): A monastic college or school.

shravaka (Skt.): One who hears and proclaims the basic teachings of the Buddha. See also **shravakayana**.

shravakayana (Skt., literally, "way of the hearers"): The focus of the shravakayana is on individual salvation through listening to the teachings and gaining insight into the four noble truths and the unreality of phenomena. The shravakayana can be equated with the hinayana.

shunyata (Skt.): "Emptiness." A completely open and unbounded clarity of mind characterized by groundlessness and freedom from all conceptual frameworks. It could be called "openness" since "emptiness" can convey the mistaken notion of a state of voidness or blankness. In fact, shunyata is inseparable from compassion and all other awakened qualities.

siddha (Skt.): A realized practitioner who has accomplished siddhi, or power, over the phenomenal world and, more fundamentally, over mind itself. See also **mahasiddha**.

siddhi: See **siddha**.

six realms: Worlds that can be regarded as literal or metaphorical descriptions of existence. They are the realms of hell, hungry ghosts, animals, humans, jealous gods, and gods.

six yogas of Naropa: Also called the "six dharmas of Naropa." Advanced tantric practices that the mahasiddha Naropa transmitted, which became an essential transmission and group of practices in the Karma Kagyü and other lineages. They comprise the yoga of inner heat, dream yoga, the yoga of luminosity, the yoga of bardo, the yoga of illusory body, and the transference of consciousness.

skull cup (Skt. *kapala*): A cup that is either made from a human skull or visualized as being made from a human skull. The kapala is used in vajrayana rituals and usually contains amrita. It represents conquest over extreme beliefs or the intoxication of extreme beliefs.

stupa (Skt.): A structure or building that contains the relics of a great teacher.

tantra (Skt., literally "continuity"): A synonym for *vajrayana*, the third of the three main yanas of Tibetan Buddhism. Refers both to the root texts of the vajrayana and to the systems of meditation they describe.

thangka (Tib.): A form of Tibetan religious painting that depicts the gurus, mandalas, deities, and other iconographic aspects of the vajrayana.

Tibetan Book of the Dead, The (Tib., *Bardo Thödol*, "Book of Liberation in the Bardo through Hearing"): A famous Tibetan tantric terma text on working with death and dying and the after-death state. Chögyam Trungpa worked on a translation of *The Tibetan Book of the Dead* that is still quite popular and that makes these teachings much more accesible to Western readers through the explanation of their psychological significance. The origin of these teachings can be traced to Padmasambhava and his consort, Yeshe Tsogyal. It was later discovered as terma by Karma Lingpa in the fourteenth century. Intensively studied in Tibet, both academically and during retreat practice, the text is often read aloud to dying persons to help them attain realization within the bardo. The Surmang monasteries and the Trungpas have been associated closely with teachings from *The Tibetan Book of the Dead* for several centuries.

Tilopa: A renowned teacher of vajrayana Buddhism in India in the eleventh century. His most famous disciple was Naropa, who through his student Marpa, introduced Tilopa's teachings into Tibet.

vajra master: A guru qualified to teach the vajrayana and to train individual students in the path of tantra.

vajrayana (Skt., literally, "the diamond way" or "the indestructible vehicle"): Vajra-yana is the third of the three great yanas of Tibetan Buddhism. It is synonymous with tantra and is sometimes subdivided into four or six subsidiary yanas.

Vajrayogini (Skt.): One of the principal deities, or yidams, of the Kagyü school of Tibetan Buddhism. Vajrayogini is the consort of Chakrasamvara. She represents the principle of nonthought, or wisdom beyond conceptual mind.

vidyadhara (Skt.): A title for a vajrayana teacher, signifying a holder of wisdom, or a crazy-wisdom lineage holder. With a capital *V*, an honorific title given to Chög-yam Trungpa.

yana (Skt.): A vehicle in which, symbolically, the practitioner travels on the road to enlightenment. The different vehicles, or yanas, correspond to different views of the journey, and each yana comprises a body of knowledge and practice. The three great yanas in Tibetan Buddhism are the hinayana, mahayana, and vajrayana. See also **hinayana**, **mahayana**, and **vajrayana**.

yidams (Tib.): Vajrayana deities who embody various aspects of the awakened nature of mind.

yogin (Skt.): A tantric practitioner, or more generally a practitioner of yoga. Used in both Buddhist and Hindu tantra. A yogini is a female tantric practitioner.

Resources

OCEAN OF DHARMA QUOTES OF THE WEEK brings you the teachings of Chögyam Trungpa Rinpoche. An e-mail is sent out several times each week containing a quote from Chögyam Trungpa's extensive teachings. Quotations of material may be from unpublished material, forthcoming publications, or previously published sources. Ocean of Dharma Quotes of the Week are selected by Carolyn Rose Gimian. To enroll, go to www.oceanofdharma.com.

For information regarding meditation instruction, please visit the website of Shambhala International at www.shambhala.org. This website contains information about the more than one hundred centers affiliated with Shambhala.

The Chögyam Trungpa Legacy Project was established to help preserve, disseminate, and expand Chögyam Trungpa's legacy. The Legacy Project supports the preservation, propagation, and publication of Trungpa Rinpoche's dharma teachings. This includes plans for the creation of a comprehensive virtual archive and learning community. For information, go to www.chogyamtrungpa.com.

For publications from Vajradhatu Publications and Kalapa Recordings, including both books and audiovisual materials, go to www.shambhalashop.com.

For information about the archive of the author's work, please contact the Shambhala Archives: archives@shambhala.org.

The Konchok Foundation is dedicated to helping meet the spiritual, cultural, educational, and humanitarian needs of the Tibetan people in Sur-mang and elsewhere in the Kham and Golok regions of Tibet. For further information, go to www.konchok.org.

About the Author

THE VENERABLE CHÖGYAM TRUNGPA RINPOCHE was born in the province of Kham in eastern Tibet in 1940. When he was just thirteen months old, Chögyam Trungpa was recognized as a major tulku, or incarnate teacher. According to Tibetan tradition, an enlightened teacher is capable, based on his or her vow of compassion, of reincarnating in human form over a succession of generations. Before dying, such a teacher may leave a letter or other clues to the whereabouts of the next incarnation. Later, students and other realized teachers look through these clues and, based on those, plus a careful examination of dreams and visions, conduct searches to discover and recognize the successor. Thus, particular lines of teaching are formed, in some cases extending over many centuries. Chögyam Trungpa was the eleventh in the teaching lineage known as the Trungpa Tulkus.

Once young tulkus are recognized, they enter a period of intensive training in the theory and practice of the Buddhist teachings. Trungpa Rinpoche, after being enthroned as supreme abbot of Surmang Dütsi Tel Monastery and governor of Surmang District, began a period of training that would last eighteen years, until his departure from Tibet in 1959. As a Kagyü tulku, his training was based on the systematic practice of meditation and on refined theoretical understanding of Buddhist philosophy. One of the four great lineages of Tibet, the Kagyü is known as the Practicing (or Practice) Lineage.

At the age of eight, Trungpa Rinpoche received ordination as a novice monk. Following this, he engaged in intensive study and practice of the traditional monastic disciplines, including traditional Tibetan poetry and monastic dance. His primary teachers were Jamgön Kongtrül of Sechen and Khenpo Gangshar—leading teachers in the Nyingma and Kagyü lineages. In 1958, at the age of eighteen, Trungpa Rinpoche completed his studies, receiving the degrees of kyorpön (doctor of divinity) and khenpo (master of studies). He also received full monastic ordination.

The late fifties was a time of great upheaval in Tibet. As it became clear that the Chinese Communists intended to take over the country by force, many people, both monastic and lay, fled the country. Trungpa Rinpoche spent many harrowing months trekking over the Himalayas (described later in his book *Born in Tibet*). After narrowly escaping capture by the Chinese, he at last reached India in 1959. While in India, Trungpa Rinpoche was appointed to serve as spiritual adviser to the Young Lamas Home School in Delhi, India. He served in this capacity from 1959 to 1963.

Trungpa Rinpoche's opportunity to emigrate to the West came when he received a Spalding sponsorship to attend Oxford University. At Oxford he studied comparative religion, philosophy, history, and fine arts. He also studied Japanese flower arranging, receiving a degree from the Sogetsu School. While in England, Trungpa Rinpoche began to instruct Western students in the dharma, and in 1967 he founded the Samye Ling Meditation Center in Dumfriesshire, Scotland. During this period, he also published his first two books, both in English: *Born in Tibet* (1966) and *Meditation in Action* (1969).

In 1968 Trungpa Rinpoche traveled to Bhutan, where he entered into a solitary meditation retreat. While on retreat, Rinpoche received a pivotal terma text for all of his teaching in the West, "The Sadhana of Mahamudra," a text that documents the spiritual degeneration of modern times and its antidote, genuine spirituality that leads to the experience of naked and luminous mind. This retreat marked a pivotal change in his approach to teaching. Soon after returning to England, he became a layperson, putting aside his monastic robes and dressing in ordinary Western attire. In 1970 he married a young Englishwoman, Diana Pybus, and together they left Scotland and moved to North America. Many of his early students and his Tibetan colleagues found these changes shocking and upsetting. However, he expressed a conviction that in order for the dharma to take root in the West, it needed to be taught free from cultural trappings and religious fascination.

During the seventies, America was in a period of political and cultural ferment. It was a time of fascination with the East. Nevertheless, almost from the moment he arrived in America, Trungpa Rinpoche drew many students to him who were seriously interested in the Buddhist teachings and the practice of meditation. However, he severely criticized the materialistic approach to spirituality that was also quite prevalent, describing it as a "spiritual supermarket." In his lectures, and in his books *Cutting Through Spiritual Materialism* (1973) and *The Myth of Freedom* (1976), he pointed to the simplicity and directness of the practice of sitting meditation as the way to cut through such distortions of the spiritual journey.

During his seventeen years of teaching in North America, Trungpa Rinpoche developed a reputation as a dynamic and controversial teacher. He was a pioneer, one of the first Tibetan Buddhist teachers in North America, preceding by some years and indeed facilitating the later visits by His Holiness the Karmapa, His Holiness Khyentse Rinpoche, His Holiness the Dalai Lama, and many others. In the United States, he found a spiritual kinship with many Zen masters, who were already presenting Buddhist meditation. In the very early days, he particularly connected with Suzuki Roshi, the founder of Zen Center in San Francisco. In later years he was close with Kobun Chino Roshi and Bill Kwong Roshi in Northern California; with Maezumi Roshi, the founder of the Los Angeles Zen Center; and with Eido Roshi, abbot of the New York Zendo Shobo-ji.

Fluent in the English language, Chögyam Trungpa was one of the first Tibetan Buddhist teachers who could speak to Western students directly, without the aid of a translator. Traveling extensively throughout North America and Europe, he gave thousands of talks and hundred of seminars. He established major centers in Vermont, Colorado, and Nova Scotia, as well as many smaller meditation and study centers in cities throughout North America and Europe. Vajradhatu was formed in 1973 as the central administrative body of this network.

In 1974 Trungpa Rinpoche founded the Naropa Institute (now Naropa University), which became the first and only accredited Buddhist-inspired university in North America. He lectured extensively at the institute, and his book *Journey without Goal* (1981) is based on a course he taught there. In 1976 he established the Shambhala Training program, a series of seminars that present a nonsectarian path of spiritual warriorship grounded in the practice of sitting meditation. His book *Shambhala: The Sacred Path of the Warrior* (1984) gives an overview of the Shambhala teachings.

In 1976 Trungpa Rinpoche appointed Ösel Tendzin (Thomas F. Rich) as his Vajra Regent, or dharma heir. Ösel Tendzin worked closely with Trungpa Rinpoche in the administration of Vajradhatu and Shambhala Training. He taught extensively from 1976 until his death in 1990 and is the author of *Buddha in the Palm of Your Hand*.

Trungpa Rinpoche was also active in the field of translation. Working with Francesca Fremantle, he rendered a new translation of *The Tibetan Book of the Dead*, which was published in 1975. Later he formed the Nalanda Translation Committee in order to translate texts and liturgies for his own students as well as to make important texts available publicly.

In 1979 Trungpa Rinpoche conducted a ceremony empowering his eldest son, Ösel Rangdröl Mukpo, as his successor in the Shambhala lineage. At that time he gave him the title of Sawang ("Earth Lord").

Trungpa Rinpoche was also known for his interest in the arts and particularly for his insights into the relationship between contemplative discipline and the artistic process. Two books published since his death—*The Art of Calligraphy* (1994) and *Dharma Art* (1996) [a new edition appeared in 2008 under the title *True Perception: The Path of Dharma Art*]—present this aspect of his work. His own artwork included calligraphy, painting, flower arranging, poetry, playwriting, and environmental installations. In addition, at the Naropa Institute he created an educational atmosphere that attracted many leading artists and poets. The exploration of the creative process in light of contemplative training continues there as a provocative dialogue. Trungpa Rinpoche also published two books of poetry: *Mudra* (1972) and *First Thought Best Thought* (1983). In 1998 a retrospective compilation of his poetry, *Timely Rain*, was published.

Shortly before his death, in a meeting with Samuel Bercholz, the publisher of Shambhala Publications, Chögyam Trungpa expressed his interest in publishing 108 volumes of his teachings, to be called the Dharma Ocean Series. "Dharma Ocean" is the translation of Chögyam Trungpa's Tibetan teaching name, Chökyi Gyatso. The Dharma Ocean Series was to consist primarily of material edited to allow readers to encounter this rich array of teachings simply and directly rather than in an overly systematized or condensed form. In 1991 the first posthumous volume in the series, *Crazy Wisdom*, was published, and another seven volumes followed in the ensuing years. Plans continue for many future volumes of his teachings to be published.

Trungpa Rinpoche's published books represent only a fraction of the rich legacy of his teachings. During his seventeen years of teaching in North America, he crafted the structures necessary to provide his students with thorough, systematic training in the dharma. From introductory talks and courses to advanced group retreat practices, these programs emphasized a balance of study and practice, of intellect and intuition. *Chögyam Trungpa* by Fabrice Midal, a biography, details the many forms of training that Chögyam Trungpa developed. *Dragon Thunder: My Life with Chögyam Trungpa,* is the story of Rinpoche's life as told by Diana Mukpo. This also provides insight into the many forms that he crafted for Buddhism in North America.

In addition to his extensive teachings in the Buddhist tradition, Trungpa Rinpoche also placed great emphasis on the Shambhala teachings, which stress the importance of meditation in action, synchronizing mind and body, and training oneself to approach obstacles or challenges in everyday life with the courageous attitude of a warrior, without anger. The goal of creating an enlightened society is fundamental to the Shambhala teachings. According to the Shambhala approach, the realization of an enlightened society comes not purely through outer activity, such as community or political involvement, but from appreciation of the senses and the sacred dimension of day-to-day life. A second volume of these teachings, entitled *Great Eastern Sun*, was published in 1999. The final volume of these teachings, *Smile at Fear*, will appear in 2009.

Chögyam Trungpa died in 1987, at the age of forty-seven. By the time of his death, he was known not only as Rinpoche ("Precious Jewel") but also as Vajracharya ("Vajra Holder") and as Vidyadhara ("Wisdom Holder") for his role as a master of the vajrayana, or tantric teachings of Buddhism. As a holder of the Shambhala teachings, he had also received the titles of

Dorje Dradül ("Indestructible Warrior") and Sakyong ("Earth Protector").
He is survived by his wife, Diana Judith Mukpo, and five sons. His eldest
son, the Sawang Ösel Rangdröl Mukpo, succeeds him as the spiritual head
of Vajradhatu. Acknowledging the importance of the Shambhala teachings
to his father's work, the Sawang changed the name of the umbrella organization to Shambhala, with Vajradhatu remaining one of its major divisions.
In 1995 the Sawang received the Shambhala title of Sakyong like his father
before him and was also confirmed as an incarnation of the great ecumeni-
cal teacher Mipham Rinpoche.

Trungpa Rinpoche is widely acknowledged as a pivotal figure in intro-
ducing the buddhadharma to the Western world. He joined his great
appreciation for Western culture with his deep understanding of his own
tradition. This led to a revolutionary approach to teaching the dharma, in
which the most ancient and profound teachings were presented in a thoroughly contemporary way. Trungpa Rinpoche was known for his fearless
proclamation of the dharma: free from hesitation, true to the purity of the
tradition, and utterly fresh. May these teachings take root and flourish for
the benefit of all sentient beings.

Index

Also by Chögyam Trungpa

Born in Tibet

Cutting Through Spiritual Materialism

Great Eastern Sun

The Heart of the Buddha

Journey without Goal

Meditation in Action

The Myth of Freedom and the Way
of Meditation

Ocean of Dharma

The Path Is the Goal

The Sanity We Are Born With

Shambhala: The Sacred Path of the Warrior

Training the Mind and Cultivating
Loving-Kindness